SENTINEL

SENTINEL

Become the Agent in Charge of Your Own Protection Detail

PATRICK MCNAMARA

iUniverse, Inc.
Bloomington

SENTINEL
Become the Agent in Charge of Your Own Protection Detail

iUniverse books may be ordered through booksellers or by contacting:

iUniverse
1663 Liberty Drive
Bloomington, IN 47403
www.iuniverse.com
1-800-Authors (1-800-288-4677)

ISBN: 978-1-4759-6049-5 (sc)
ISBN: 978-1-4759-6050-1 (ebk)

Library of Congress Control Number: 2012921694

Printed in the United States of America

iUniverse rev. date: 11/27/2012

Contents

As defined by Dictionary.com:

Sentinel • sen·ti·nel

1. a person or thing that watches or stands as if watching.
2. a soldier stationed as a guard to challenge all comers and prevent a surprise attack: *to stand sentinel.*
3. Also called <u>tag.</u> *Computers.* a symbol, mark, or other labeling device indicating the beginning or end of a unit of information.
   —*verb (used with object)*
4. to watch over or guard as a sentinel.

Origin: 1570-80; < MF *sentinelle* < It *sentinella,* deriv. of OIt *sentina* vigilance (L *sent(īre)* to observe) +*-īna-*<u>ine2</u>)

Introduction

We may not be able to plan for everything that is uncertain in life, but we are capable of increasing our levels of awareness and preparedness. Economic collapse, storms of biblical proportions, and zombie attacks are not as likely as unfortunate events that happen in our day-to-day existence. There are simple steps we may take to assist us in being better prepared for power blackouts, home invasion, and attacks on the street from random dirtbags.

We should enjoy relative peace of mind knowing that we have planned for uncertainty, and we should rest easier at the top of the food chain. It is said that information is power. It may also be powerful and able to arm us with increased levels of lethality and survivability.

At the very least, increasing the scope of our capabilities database is a battlefield multiplier on the front lines of life.

Take Back
Your Sentinel Authority

Anything can happen to anyone, anywhere, at any time. It's called Murphy's Law. That being said, wouldn't you rather know that you had done everything in your power to have prepared yourself for that Murphy's Moment? None of us plan to fail. We may, however, fail to plan.

I served in the military for twenty-two years, and in that time never left the special operations community. I've been battered, broken, and bruised but have also enjoyed the sweet taste of success as I toiled through some of the military's toughest training. I descended from skyscrapers and ran through breach points consumed by fire. I jumped from aircraft at heights where the curvature of the earth was visible. I have flown into hostile territory on the outside of rotary-winged aircraft. I have tangled with some of the planet's biggest and most notorious villains. I set up spy networks in Eastern Europe during the Cold War and spied on the Soviet Army when spying was face-to-face, not in cyberspace. I had to discern, discriminate, formulate, and act in nanoseconds.

There was a time when I was human with immortal qualities. I was a creature of the night and a harvester of souls. I was one of our country's agents of correction. I oozed attitude and fortitude. I have protected generals, dignitaries, heads of state, and royalty.

1

Fast-forward to today where I have a less-than-arduous task list: I must assist in a school field trip. I am packing lunches with PB & Js, juice boxes, and fruit roll-ups. Mmmm . . . fruit roll-ups. At times I feel as though someone stepped on my Man-Card.

I have a new mission now, that's all, and it includes PB & Js and PTAs. It is a mission of self-preservation and force-preservation. The force, in this case, is my family. I must embrace this new mission, as it is my duty as a human being and duty as a rational human. I must count on myself to protect myself and my family. This mission was not assigned to me, but rather it is a God-given duty. I have the tools necessary to accomplish this mission within me. I must access my data bank's primal side. I am a human being and was born with natural defense mechanisms. I must give my mind permission to allow these mechanisms to work automatically.

We humans and our descendants have been on this planet for a couple million years. We are not hunting mammoths or dodging saber-toothed tigers anymore, but dangers still lurk in the shadows. We must safeguard ourselves and our families. Self-preservation must be front and center. If we are the head of a family, priorities shift, but we must preserve the self in order to preserve *the force*.

I am the *agent in charge* of my own protective detail. The *AIC*. I am the protector and the *protectee*. I have a wife and children. It is my responsibility to protect them. I am not a bodyguard. I am my family's Batman. I am the shepherd of my flock.

I am a Sentinel.

Your Protection Detail

The group of professionals assigned to a protectee, or *principal*, is called a *protection detail*. The term *executive protection* was coined in the 1970s by the United States Secret Service when they created the Executive Protection Service to guard visiting foreign dignitaries.

The protection of an individual is comprehensive and goes well beyond surrounding the individual with well-armed agents. As part of an *executive protection detail*'s mission of preventing an incident before it occurs, the detail relies on meticulous advance work and threat assessments developed by its Intelligence Division to identify potential risks to principals.

So let us discuss, in a nutshell, how a protection detail is put together and how it operates.

First off, the difference between a bodyguard and a protection professional is that a bodyguard is a goon in a suit and specializes in knuckle dragging. A protection professional typically works on an executive protection detail and is better prepared to process information in the environment, identify threats before they materialize, and then formulate a variety of courses of action.

An executive protection detail is a complex machine requiring several necessary moving components. There are motorcade operations, including a lead car in front and a follow car in back of the dignitary's limo; advance operations; inner and outer circles; a chain of command that includes an agent in charge (AIC) and a shift leader (SL), pre-posted and counter-surveillance agents; and the list goes on.

Executive protection (EP), also known as close personal protection, refers to security measures taken to ensure the safety of VIPs or other individuals who may be exposed to elevated personal risk because of their employment, celebrity status, wealth, associations, or geographical location. It is a highly specialized field within the private security industry. Elite executive protection professionals (aka *agents*) will have specialized training in executive protection, driving, first aid, and marksmanship.

The primary purpose of an EP detail is to safeguard the principal from harm and from situations likely to endanger his or her person or liberty (i.e., murder, manslaughter, willful threats to kill, extortion, kidnapping, and/or assault). Today, the principal is *you*; it is your girlfriend, your wife, your kids, your elderly parents.

The secondary purpose of an EP detail is to safeguard the principal from harassment or embarrassment. Most likely this will involve prevention of heckling, soiling of clothes, or bodily injury. At no time must the level of protection diminish.

Many times the principal will be in a difficult situation. If the principal wishes to be shielded from public view, the detail must honor his or her wishes.

In your protection detail, you are the AIC, and your kids or significant other become the principal. If you have a family, your safety comes second to theirs.

You Are the Agent in Charge (AIC)

Executive protection is an atrocious job. There is nothing glamorous about it. It is not sexy. It is not about being a gunslinger or about muscle flexing. It is exhausting, frustrating, and taxing. When living in someone's hip pocket, you must anticipate that person's every move, think one step ahead of that person. You must forecast, predict, anticipate. Your gears may never stop turning. You must protect your principal from his or her enemies. You must ensure that your principal does not become his or her own worst enemy. You must remain eternally vigilant.

The AIC has to be an expert in protective security. He or she plans, administers, and supervises the protection detail. This is your job, whether protecting yourself or your family.

On an *executive* protection detail, the AIC maintains a liaison with the VIP principal's staff to ensure the timely exchange of information regarding schedule, threat, unscheduled moves, etc. The AIC assigns agents to specific shifts and supervisory positions (i.e., close-in body cover) prior to the *onset of detail*—when the protection begins. He or she has a relationship with the principal but maintains a formal demeanor—the AIC must be adaptable to the principal's style, which includes establishing rapport, but can never lose sight of the environment.

The AIC must provide close-in cover as a number-one priority. When dealing with the rest of the detail, he or she must use discretion in assignments, delegating when appropriate and considering grade, experience, attitude, knowledge, and demeanor. The AIC may not display favoritism and accepts responsibility for the conduct of the agents assigned as well as the conduct of the detail in general.

The AIC is ultimately responsible for all equipment, which includes radio/communications equipment, vehicles, weapons and ammunition, special protective equipment (CS gas, ballistic raincoat, riot helmets, federal packs/blue lights, etc.), medical equipment, and support equipment (flashlights, parkas, rain gear, maps, pry bar, automotive equipment, etc.).

The AIC rides in the right front seat of the limousine with the principal.

On your protection detail, you are not only the AIC—responsible for the vehicles and the routes, both primary and secondary, as well as making sure that all weapons are accounted for, loaded, and in the proper carry position—you are also the limo driver. That means it's your job to ensure that the vehicle is clean inside and out, check the vehicle's mechanical condition (i.e., oil, fluids, belts, wipers, lights, flashers, and horns); test all doors and locks, and ask for assistance if unfamiliar with an item or its use. You must account for all emergency equipment and verify that it's functioning. And you must drive to save your life or the life of your principal if necessary.

On your protection detail, you have additional roles. You are the shift leader (SL), who is the first-line supervisor and tactical commander, and you also assume the duties of the lead- and follow-car drivers who must advise and update the driver concerning traffic conditions and advise when it is safe to make lane changes and turns. As follow-car driver (FCD) you must keep the tactical radio on and be the radio operator. The tactical radio in this case, is your cell phone.

You will also have a special role at the command post (CP or *home*) where you must assume residence watch (RW) and continue to monitor tactical radios and telephone communications.

If the protection detail needs assistance in either an emergency or nonemergency situation, you must notify the appropriate authorities and continue to monitor the situation via radio. *Always* monitor the detail's radio traffic and *anticipate* any assistance that the detail may require. That means you maintain the security of the residence when the principals are not present. You are ultimately responsible for the operation of the command post.

As the advance agent, you have to be the security expert for the site. The advance agent has vast and various responsibilities with regard to the planning and establishment of security measures at a site to be visited by the principal. These responsibilities will be covered in a separate chapter.

Limo Driver

In the 1980s, I was a member of two different Cold War–era military units. The United States Military Liaison Mission (USMLM) was one of them. The USMLM collected intelligence "on the ground" on the Soviet and East German militaries and contributed to the fall of the Soviet empire in ways few people know.

One of the prerequisites required of me for this position was to attend the German Federal Intelligence Service driving school or Bundesnachrichtendienst Fahrschule. This was the first of many driving schools provided to me while serving in the military. I've also been to Rod Hall Racing, a NASCAR school at the Gateway Speedway; BSR (Bill Scott Racing); and the Gary Semics Motocross School.

Armed with a highly modified Mercedes Gelandewagan, topographical maps, recent satellite intelligence, and the latest in still and video recording devices, we would cross West Berlin's Freedom Bridge with our cover-for-action credentials to prowl the vast network of dirt roads that connected hundreds of training areas that were scattered about Soviet East Germany.

Other prerequisites to working in the USMLM included speaking either German or Russian. One had to be a WPID (WARSAW Pact Identification) expert and be an expert driver. Expert driving skills proved necessary when evading the ever-vigilant Stasi or the *Ministerium für Staatssicherheit* (Ministry for State Security). The Stasi was widely regarded as one of the most effective and repressive intelligence and secret police agencies in the world.

We had to evade agile armored vehicles such as BTR 70s, T-80s, and BMP2s. BMPs were like the Velociraptors of the armored vehicle world. On the paved roads, monster-sized troop carriers like Zil131s and URAL 4320s would consider us the flavor of the day. It was one big game of cat and mouse, and we had to be on our toes.

On your protection detail, you will probably not have to evade hostiles belonging to a Communist superpower, but the scope of an adversary is all relative when your family's safety is at issue.

On an executive protection detail, the limo driver prepares to move at a moment's notice. He or she ensures safe and comfortable transport. The driver must know the vehicle inside and out.

Whether you drive a Honda Civic or a Chevy Suburban, your vehicle is your *mobile command center*. The driver should know *all* primary and secondary routes to and from home and destination and all emergency routes, such as hospitals and safe havens. The driver should drive all the routes in daylight as well as nighttime to become familiar with them, keeping in mind that landmarks look different at night.

In an EP detail, the driver ensures the vehicle is clean inside and out, checks the vehicle's mechanical condition—oil, tires, power steering fluid, belts, radiator fluid, wipers, brake lights, flashers, headlights, and horn. And you should keep your car in tiptop shape at all times as well. This is your emergency escape and response vehicle; if it's not ready for an emergency, you aren't.

Make sure you keep a current account for all emergency equipment and can verify it is functioning. If you keep weapons in your house, vehicle, or on your person, ensure these are accounted for, loaded, and in the proper carry position—safe from unauthorized use by either an assailant or your child. Test all doors and automatic locks, and ask if you are unfamiliar with any item or its use.

In an EP detail, the driver ensures that the vehicle log is present and filled out and notes any problems with vehicle.

The driver sets the vehicle up thirty minutes prior to scheduled departure.

He or she starts the vehicle's engine fifteen minutes prior to scheduled departure.

He or she knows the motorcade route (even if there is a lead vehicle), so that the motorcade may continue if the lead car is lost. There must be *no* surprises. The driver cannot react to danger if he or she does not know what situations are right or wrong.

The driver safeguards the car keys. When the vehicle is not in use, it should be locked and its keys kept inside the command post. A spare set should be kept in the follow car.

On your protection detail you assume the duties of the lead, limo, and follow cars. You must be prepared to depart at a moment's notice. Your vehicle should be washed and gassed at all times. Don't get yourself caught in a self-induced Murphy's Moment. My rule is that while in the driveway, the fuel gauge never reads less than three quarters of a tank.

When driving, *drive to save your life*. Drive defensively and be prepared to drive offensively when necessary. When behind the wheel, life is a chess match. Pay attention at all times. Be relentless. Do not focus your attention only on what is directly in front of you. Perform a focal shift to see things full spectrum.

> *Driving defensively means driving to save lives, time, and money, in spite of the conditions around you and the actions of others.*

This definition is taken from the National Safety Council's Defensive Driving Course. It is a form of training for motor vehicle drivers that goes beyond mastery of the rules of the road and the basic mechanics of driving. Its aim is to reduce the risk of driving by anticipating dangerous situations, despite adverse conditions or the mistakes of others. This can be achieved through adherence to a variety of general rules, as well as the practice of specific driving techniques.

- Take heed and forecast potential chokepoints. Chokepoints can be defined as any place that you cannot easily get out of.
- Prior to entering an intersection, select your lane based on mobility. Mobility equals survivability.
  - o Always allow yourself an out.

11

o Never close in on the vehicle in front of you at a stop light. Allow yourself a reactionary gap of at least one vehicle length.

o If the intersection has multiple lanes, try to stop in the outside lane to give yourself an additional egress route.

Visualize jumping the curb. Visualize slamming the shifter into reverse and smoking your tires. Visualize the chaos. Hear the tires squeal and smell the smoke. If you picture yourself doing it, you have conducted a dry run. You are now more prepared to react in the event you must react.

- When on a two-way road where posted speed limits read 55 mph, your life rests in the hands of the drivers coming toward you in the opposite lane. Can you trust them? We are all human. Any one of those drivers can doze off, get distracted, or have a vehicular malfunction. I am intermittently looking for an out on my side of the road, and so should you.

- A responsible driver will not talk on his or her cell phone while on duty. This includes hands-free cell phones. Here is a news flash for you: we human beings are not capable of multitasking. None of us are.

Consciously concentrating on two involved tasks at the same time, especially under stress, is mentally impossible. There are only workarounds (task switching and stacking) that typically lead to the degradation of one task or the other. The time required to switch can be reduced through repetition and practiced motion, or one task can be trained to a level of unconscious competence (why we can walk and chew bubble gum).

> *Multitasking, when it comes to paying attention, is a myth. The brain naturally focuses on concepts sequentially, one at a time. At first that might sound confusing; at one level the brain does multitask. You can walk and talk at the same time. Your brain controls your heartbeat while you read a book. A pianist can play a piece with left and right hand simultaneously. Surely this is multitasking. But I am talking about the brain's ability to pay attention . . . To put it bluntly, research shows that we can't multitask. We are biologically incapable of processing attention-rich inputs simultaneously.*

> —John Medina, *Brain Rules*

When you are out of town on business and in charge of your *personal* security detail, dry rehearse your rental car. Run through a *battle drill* of sorts several times and do this before you leave the parking lot of the rental car agency:

- Think of worst-case scenarios where mobility ends and must be regained via your feet. Your car is stuck on the railroad tracks, for instance. Start with your hands on the wheel. Give yourself a countdown: *3, 2, 1, go.* Unbuckle your seat belt, open the door, scan the immediate area, get out, and move away from the vehicle.

This is called an *immediate action drill*. IADs are performed numerous times to assure that certain actions can be performed immediately at near-subconscious level. This drill may seem rudimentary, but I bet you have found yourself in a vehicle that did not belong to you and you had to search for the door handle. If it was dark, this search frustrated you. I am betting that you have searched for a door handle in an unfamiliar vehicle. Do not become a victim due to loss of mobility. If you lose mobility because of something horrible happening, you must regain mobility via your hoofers. Why? *Mobility equals survivability.*

Consider other factors that could limit your mobility. Does your car have those Jeffrey-Dahmer-serial-killer automatic locks that go *THUMP* when you put it into gear? Does the tilt steering limit your egress? If you cannot get out of your vehicle while it is stuck on the railroad tracks, you might be shit out of luck. You don't want to be thinking, *I should have practiced that drill . . .*

Ditching Procedure (Bridge Example)

Talk yourself and talk your family through your ditching procedures. For example, this is what I do prior to driving over any water-spanning bridges:

- Close all windows and the sunroof. I would need my vehicle to float for as long as possible. We will make a determination to open a window and exit if we are floating, and deem it safe. If it is not safe to do so, I will brief them to wait until the windows and doors are completely submerged before opening them. Number one, they will be nearly impossible to open until the pressure is equalized. Panic may set in when fighting hundreds of square-foot pounds. Number two, if one rolls the window down before completely submerged, water will rush in like a torrent, again creating panic that will cloud clear thinking and have dire results.

- I want my family to keep their seatbelts on until after impact, and then remove them immediately. So we practice that action of quickly removing the belts.

Parking Lots

Parking is another risk area, so establish a parking routine. Think about your egress when you park. Backing in not only provides a better exit, but mitigates the possibility of would-be scammers waiting in your blind spot while you back out. "WHAM!" Lawsuit!

Before you climb out of your vehicle, take a look around and look in depth, noting shadows and corners. It only takes a second to scan your primary and secondary sectors. Your primary is directly outside of your vehicle and your secondary runs two or three cars deep in all directions. Just spend a couple of seconds on this. Make it your new normal. You will be surprised at what you see. If something makes you uncomfortable or doesn't fit, leave or move so you can live to fight another day. The best way to get out of a sticky situation is by not getting into it in the first place.

Once out of the vehicle, plan your walking route to your destination and check to ensure you have your car keys. I have mine on a small snap link and have made it a habit to secure my keys to a belt loop. I check the keys prior to shutting the car door. This is a habit of mine. An ounce of prevention . . .

Conduct the same scan prior to walking to your car in the parking lot from the relative safety of the mall or shopping center. Make this a new normal. Turn it into a routine. If you do it enough, you will do it intuitively. This task will rest in your subconscious mind, and you will access the task whenever you need it.

If you feel you are being followed in your car as you are approaching your neighborhood, conduct a surveillance detection route (SDR). An SDR is a Cold War relic that a spy would use to determine the identification of a potential adversary, and it might serve to tell you whether or not paranoia has set in. If it hasn't, the SDR can deter would-be adversaries from pinpointing the location of your residence. Do not drive past your house unless you have already reached the point of no return. Take your new friend on a tour of the neighborhood. If you have no doubt that you have picked up a tail and that he or she is unrelenting, drive to your nearest government place of business like a post office, fire station, or police station and look for a trusted agent.

Know Your & Your Vehicle's Limits

If you really want to understand the dynamics of your vehicle, I would recommend attending a course that offers *swerve-to-avoid* maneuvers at highway speeds; drills on how to focus your attention on a positive goal such as an escape route, rather than a problem such as a tree or another vehicle; drills focusing on vehicle dynamics and feedback, skid-control-and-recovery practice on a dedicated skid pad and on a slalom course; threshold braking on straightaways and progressive braking on curves; and off-road recovery.

Only once you have discovered how far you can take a vehicle, will you be confident enough to take it there while under duress.

Fix It Yourself

It may seem intimidating, but basic car care is often simply a matter of popping open the hood and taking a look at the engine of your vehicle. Easier still, it starts with examining the exterior. Check your tires at least every other week to make sure they are inflated properly. This should be an actual check with a tire pressure gauge, but even a visual check to make sure the tires appear equally and properly inflated, have retained their tread, and are free of cracks will put you at an advantage.

Of course, much of the day-to-day driving maintenance for your vehicle must occur with the hood opened and up, but that doesn't mean you have to be a mechanic. The most important things to monitor and check regularly include the following:

- engine oil level and cleanliness
- antifreeze/coolant level (never attempt to remove radiator cap while engine is hot or warm)
- brake and power-steering fluid levels
- transmission
- fluid belts

You should also keep an eye on your vehicle's battery, and be aware of its age. Batteries should be replaced every five years or so, and if your battery is not getting the proper charge to easily start your car, you should have it checked. You can usually have your battery's charge and water level checked for free at a battery replacement station. Most vehicle batteries come with comprehensive warranties, as well.

The biggest thing to remember with ongoing vehicle maintenance is to address issues promptly, including engine knocking or other noises, and do your best to try to understand what may be going on before you visit the mechanic.

Flat tires are a fact of life. Tires are made of rubber and therefore can be punctured; there is little anyone can do to prevent this. We can however be prepared to face the eventuality. Everyone should have a spare tire, a can of Fix-A-Flat-type emergency sealant, and a tire-plug kit in their vehicle. A plug kit will help you make a near-permanent repair to your tire in the field, depending on what kind of flat you have.

If you happen to have a flat while away from your home and are not confident in being able to plug the tire, you should install the spare tire and try plugging the flat once you return home. Using a plug kit generally requires that you have access to compressed air in order to reinflate your tire once it has been plugged; portable 12v compressors are handy for this.

The plug can be applied to the tire while it is mounted on the vehicle if you are able to reach the damaged area—you must stabilize the vehicle with your jack first, since the tire will be losing air pressure and the pluggable wound may be anywhere. It can be dangerous to plug the tire while the car is suspended by a jack, so I recommend you remove the tire for the repair, making the damaged area easier to get to and therefore easier to apply the plug correctly. Besides being safer.

If you have sidewall damage, go straight to the spare and take the tire to a repair shop to be evaluated. The sidewall of a tire is much weaker than the tread and often will not properly hold a plug. Only use the canned Fix-A-Flat-type repair in an emergency when you cannot or do not feel safe trying another repair method; the material in the can is generally flammable and messy to remove.

Change Your Tire

Step 1: Choose your spot well.
- Pull off the road so that you are safely out of the flow of traffic.
- Try to stop in a straight part of the road, so that passing traffic can see you from a distance.
- Stop the car on a level spot; it is unsafe to jack up a car on an incline.
- Turn on your hazard lights.
- Engage the emergency brake.

Step 2: Remove tools from the vehicle.
- Retrieve all of the tools necessary: spare tire, jack, tire iron (crow bar/lug wrench), screw driver, warning cones or flares, blocks, work gloves.
- If desired, put on the gloves, and place the blocks under the tire *opposite the flat*.
- Set your warning cones or flares ten or fifteen feet behind the car to alert oncoming traffic that you are in the road.

Step 3: Prepare the tire for removal.
- Loosen the lug nuts.
- Remove the hubcap, if necessary (*some cars won't have hubcaps—consult your owner's manual for proper instructions in removing the hubcaps*).
- Using the lug wrench, begin to loosen the lug nuts (*sometimes the lug nuts are quite difficult to loosen; if you can't loosen them, try jumping on the lug wrench or lengthening it with a pipe for leverage to loosen them*).
- DO NOT REMOVE THE LUG NUTS; ONLY LOOSEN THEM.

Step 4: Jack up the vehicle.
- Consult your owners' manual and determine where the jack needs to be positioned to lift the car properly.
- Position the jack under the car and raise the jack until it contacts the frame.
- Make sure the jack is properly positioned.
- Extend the jack until the tire is about 6 inches off the ground.

Step 5: Remove the flat tire.
- Remove the lug nuts from the bolts and put them aside where you can easily retrieve them again (inside the hubcap is a common choice).
- Grab the wheel with both hands.
- Pull the wheel straight toward you and off the car.

Step 6: Put on the spare tire.
- Position the spare tire on the ground directly in front of the wheel well.
- Align the holes in the center of the spare tire with the bolts on the car.
- Lift the spare tire and position it onto the threaded bolts.
- Push the tire onto the car until it cannot go any farther.
- Replace the lug nuts on the bolts and tighten them, but not too tight—just enough to hold the tire in place while you lower the car.

Step 7: Lower the vehicle.
- Lower the car with the jack until the car is again resting on all four tires.
- Tighten the lug nuts in a star pattern, starting with one, then moving to the one opposite it, and so on. Make sure the lug nuts are nice and secure but not so tight that your wife or teenaged driver could not loosen them if need be.
- Snap the hubcap back on or put it in the trunk with your tools.

Step 8: Put the tools away.
- Place the flat tire where the spare was located.
- Replace the jack and lug wrench in their proper locations.
- Collect your cones and carefully inspect your work area to make sure that you're not leaving anything at roadside. Flashlight? Gloves? Screwdriver?

- Continue on to your destination and have the flat tire repaired.

The entire tire-changing process takes only five to ten minutes. Easier done if you have practiced the procedure before you need to do it en route.

The Advance Team

In an executive protection detail, an *advance agent* will arrive at a venue prior to the AIC and the principal. You do not have that option. You must conduct an advance on the fly. Where to sit? Where to park? What to look for directly?

If you were an advance agent, you would typically survey sites one or two days prior to a scheduled activity. If you were assigned to a high-threat detail or where large-scale security measures are needed (i.e., numerous public appearances by the principal), however, you would likely begin your survey work weeks or even months in advance.

The advance agent should be at the site at least one hour prior to the principal's arrival. The advance agent's responsibility for a given site begins when the principal departs his/her previous location en route to the site. That responsibility does not end until the principal leaves the site. However, if the advance agent has to move to advance another location before the principal leaves, the advance has to be sure to pass on all pertinent information to the shift leader and the Agent In Charge (AIC) before he or she departs.

Here are a few requirements of the advance agent. After receiving a briefing from AIC, you would complete these tasks and duties:

- Meet the detail curbside on arrival and lead them through the site.

- Review files of other site surveys.
- Arrange meetings with officials.
- Determine logistical requirements.
- Know the geographical location and have the address of the site to be visited.
- Plan the primary and secondary routes to and from the site (including an emergency departure).
- Be aware of travel time and distances to and from site.
- Know the scheduled arrival and departure times of the principal (duration of stay).
- Know the address, routes, and telephone numbers of the nearest police and fire stations for use as a safe haven, and the nearest hospital in the event of a medical emergency.
- Be aware of other elements that could interfere with the planned route (i.e., rush hour traffic, parades, demonstrations, road construction).
- Inform the protection detail of the condition of the site at intervals of five minutes and one minute out.
- Know primary and secondary routes of access and egress.
- Know emergency helicopter evacuation plans. Where and with whom is a landing zone (LZ) available, and has the crew flown into it?
- Determine motorcade arrival, departure, and staging areas.
- Know the exterior security posts.
- If practical, restrict and control access to unauthorized personnel.
- Establish barricade requirements.

- Establish parking restrictions, and if necessary, remove parked vehicles from the immediate area. EOD sweep if available.
- Establish car-stash location.
- Establish and check the principal's location, meeting rooms, etc.
- Building Configuration
  o Be familiar with floor plans (entrances, exits, elevators, roof access, basement, fire escape, stairwells)
  o Be familiar with the fire plan, firefighting equipment and systems
  o Elevators
  o Seating arrangements
- Guest Lists
  o Be familiar with guests and VIPs (number, identification, screening procedures and who by.
- Know who is in control of the keys.
- Beware of press considerations.
- Know all locations of rest rooms.
- Know all locations of holding rooms equipped with telephones.
- Know all locations of agents' security postings, down room, and refreshments.
- Know all other scheduled activities.
- Evaluate threat information.
- Establish/identify access control procedures.
- Know the role of local security.
- Select the hospital based on proximity and capabilities.

- Establish the best route to the safe haven from various locations within the site.
- Establish the best route to the limo or stash car from various locations within the site.
- Determine response time by local law enforcement, or US Military.
- Fire Response
    o Locate the nearest fire extinguisher: for what type of fire is it intended?
    o Locate all fire exits: are they all operable?
    o Does the building fire alarm automatically notify the fire department?
    o Is there an internal sprinkler system?
    o Know the location of nearest fire station, telephone number, and response time.

Holy Crap! It looks like you've got your work cut out for you.

Truthfully, you cannot be expected to perform a fraction of those tasks. There are certain things you can do on the fly however. You should have a mental checklist that you can access each time you enter a facility or establishment. We do not plan to fail, we simply fail to plan.

If I am out with my family, I am packing a pistol. If we are going to a restaurant, my checklist starts on the outside:

- Find a reference point near where you park to ensure you will remember the location.
- Look for alternative exits out of the parking lot.
- Check the time and ask yourself if it will it be dark when you exit.

Once inside,

- Scan for an alternative or emergency exit.
- Then scan each and every table. It's not about eyeballing everyone. Simply scan. You are looking for assets and liabilities.
- If you sit next to the windows, casually tap the glass. I will be asking myself, *Can I throw a table through this window? Is the table bolted down? Or will it suffice for a temporary makeshift barricade or shield?*
- Notice the foot traffic coming in and out.

I want to know if trouble is coming in, so I ask myself, *If I were a sociopath, which direction would I move after entering? Where would I aim my shotgun? What are the natural lines of drift in this establishment?*

I visualize potential chaos. Picture complete bedlam with everyone simultaneously running for the exit. This is a necessary component in preparation in the event all hell breaks loose. You must mentally prepare yourself to exit with your principals—if exiting is the best and safest recourse—*without hesitation.* Even if this means throwing the chair through the window. When pandemonium strikes, there is no time for analysis. Through analysis comes paralysis.

When I am with my family in an open-air event, like the state fair for example, I will conduct a short, clear and concise, briefing with my kiddies. They are young, so I've got to keep it simple and it must make sense to them. I will bring them to a large reference feature like a tall sign, or Ferris wheel. "This is where you come if we get separated." I might say. I will issue them a business card and tell them, "If you cannot find me, give this card to a policeman or to a mom and ask them to call me." I tell them a "mom," because kids feel naturally comfortable around mothers. And it seems moms naturally want to help a child in distress.

By the way, if I am out with my family in a public place and if you see me with shower shoes on while with my principals, please walk up to me and jam a pencil in my eye. I deserve it. Mobility equals survivability, and flip flops are not conducive to moving.

Discover Performance

The next several chapters discuss skill sets necessary to be one's own Sentinel. As you plan out your training strategy, keep in mind that limits begin where vision ends. When it comes to teaching and learning, I believe that without attitude, aptitude, and desire lives a fault line where information meets its boundary.

Whether training for street fighting, shooting, or fitness, you must believe in yourself. The mind navigates the body. In other words, how you think will determine how you perform. A positive self-image and confidence increase one's ability to perform in any area.

Your goals should be ambitious but realistic. Set short-term intermediate goals to assist you in meeting your long-term ambitious goals.

Work toward performance rather than outcome. Outcome goals are *how much*, *how many,* and *how fast.* Performance goals seek *how well.* A Sentinel's training methodology must provoke a thought process, and that's not quantitative; it's qualitative.

Your training methodology should include parameters that make your training safe, efficient, and effective. And it must encourage a continuous thought process and demand ongoing accountability.

Every professional athlete in every professional sport trains for performance over outcome. Still used today by the military and law enforcement, outcome-based training (OBT) is a performance killer. OBT is an anachronism and a failed method of instruction tried in public schools some decades ago. Unfortunately, we Americans are consumed by outcomes.

OBT is simply this: execution with consideration of the consequence. It's a running theme of "will I fail or will I succeed?" But when we are thinking about the consequence, we are not focusing on performance. Rather, we are focusing on the outcomes, and that is a performance killer.

Performance-based training (PBT) requires introspection and objective self-critique. When you think outcome, you can't help but let ego get in the way of performance. You will develop training scars and training scars can get you into trouble. Ego is a training killer. Discover performance in your Sentinel training.

We cannot control outcomes, but we can control performance. Performance is measured by doing what you can with what you have. When you are focused on the outcome, your performance will be sabotaged because you are not absorbed in the process. The probability of achieving the outcome you desire will increase once you let go of the need to have it.

I am a full-time tactical trainer. Most of my instruction revolves around firearms training. I teach a signature assault-rifle course of fire that I set up for soldiers and law enforcement officers. I call it *the scrambler*. It measures one's ability to follow instructions, come up with solutions to ambiguous situations, and to apply the fundamentals of marksmanship. It encourages planning, continuous thinking, proper bullet placement, and target discrimination.

Its setup is similar to the graphic below.

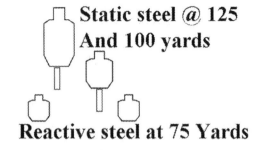

**Static steel @ 125
And 100 yards**

Reactive steel at 75 Yards

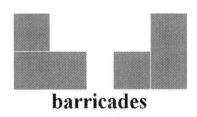

barricades

The instructions are as follows:

> *Conditions: You will wear combat kit. Your load is nine rounds distributed among three magazines: one with two, one with three, and one with four rounds loaded. The start position is ten meters from the barricades.*
>
> *Mission: You must fire at and hit an array of steel targets from two barricade positions. Static steel (steel targets that do not move when hit) and reactive steel (steel targets that fall when hit) must be shot from different barricades. You may not mix the two.*

> *On the pro-timer mark, you must assume a barricade position and engage static steel from one barricade and reactive from the other. The choice is yours.*
>
> *Two reactive targets must be engaged, one C-zone must be engaged, and you must have four hits on the iron maiden. You must apply sound tactical application when changing magazines (communicate, seek cover, weapon on safe, finger off the trigger) when moving from one barricade to another (weapon on safe, finger off the trigger, and sound off with* "moving!"*).*

I typically run this course of fire on the third day of a four-day course. It is not uncommon for me to record 100 percent failure the first-time students run the scrambler. They fail for a variety of reasons. Failure to follow instructions and too many misses top these reasons. The cause for this negative grade is simple: it is the first time in the course that the element of time has been incorporated into an event. Incorporating the element of time adds a new dimension, which is added pressure.

To the man, students are consumed by the fact that they are being timed. This thought is on the front burner. They are thinking outcome. Their brains are sabotaging their ability to perform. When one thinks outcome, he or she is letting ego get in the way of performance. Ego is a training killer.

Introspection and objective self-critique are difficult disciplines to master, with one tending to drift toward the extremes: merciless self-flagellation on one end, a stark refusal to look inward on the other. One can seesaw back and forth between both in the span of a few hours, trying to walk the line. Both these extremes are ego responses.

Before a second go at the scrambler, aptly dubbed the "Redemption Round," I discuss dismal performances with the students. I query the group on what is most important in this course of fire. They usually answer correctly. "Well-aimed shots. No misses." Additionally, we discuss how it is necessary to have the ability to *fail quickly*. In other words, do not dwell on failure. Get over it and get your head back into the game.

I ask the students to "hit control/alt/delete" to reboot the hard drive. We're not talking about computers though; we're talking about their heads. I will ask them to visualize themselves successfully running through the scrambler as seen from a helmet-camera perspective. By this time in the course, they know what is required to place well-aimed, discriminating fire on hard-to-hit targets. All they need to do now is take one shot at a time. When they hear the shot timer sound, they must hear the *beep* as permission to begin versus a race's starting signal.

The results the second time through never surprise me but always astonish those participating. Once the students give themselves permission to perform within their capability level and to focus on what is important, they record advanced results.

Train Like You Fight!

As you start on your training journey, you may . . . scratch that . . . you *will* become aware of myriad opinions, training styles, mantras, and gimmicks. Be skeptical. Some are productive battlefield multipliers. Others are crap or so watered down as to have become meaningless.

The axiom "Train like you fight" is a typical example of this: it's one of the most overused and abused axioms in the tactical training arena. I am not sure everyone knows what it means. I have had guys in training say to me that they were uncomfortable working on basic rifle marksmanship while slick (wearing no tactical gear), because it is not as they would do it in a real situation.

"But you are doing it for real" I tell them. "This is how you work the basics, and you are doing it right now . . . for real!!"

"No, I want to train like I fight," they continue.

"Okay, we will train like you fight when we start training. Right now, let's work the basics and zero our rifles, so we can get to training."

"No, if I am shooting in combat, I would be in full kit."

"Roger that. But you probably wouldn't be in a prone position, on a flat grassy range, shooting at paper targets in combat."

So what does "train like you fight" mean? Does it mean that we must train in full combat gear all of the time? Does it mean that we have to train until we drop? If it had anything to do with what we were wearing while training, then must one train in his boxer shorts if his training focus was to dissuade home invasion? Must soldiers and law enforcement train in full assault kit when they exercise? After all, they exercise to guarantee combat readiness.

I believe that training like you fight means training beyond the drill. If the drill requires six shots to complete, think seven, eight, or nine. Do not let the drill dictate to you when you should stop thinking.

I believe it means performing a *focal shift*. Check your work through your sights! See things full spectrum. Once again, work beyond the drill. If the targets are directly in front of you, look beyond in front and understand what is flanking these targets.

I believe that it means fail quickly. Do not crap yourself if your plan goes south. Get your head back in the game. Get over it. Let it roll off of you like water off of a duck's ass.

Training like this is training *how* you *want* to fight *when* you *want* to win.

Shooting 101

De-escalation techniques are the most important skills a parent can have when out with their kids—modeling good conflict resolution for one, but also for not putting gunfire in the vicinity of their principals.

In order to run an effective Sentinel detail, you should consider carrying a sidearm. It is not necessary, but it is a battlefield multiplier. If you know how to use it, it is a game changer; so get instruction. If you are carrying a sidearm, you should be doing it legally. In order to carry it legally, you will need to get a CCW permit(carrying a concealed weapon). CCW refers to the practice of carrying a handgun or other weapon in public in a concealed manner, either on one's person or in proximity.

Check online under CCW and your state to find out the particulars. You may also want to visit your neighborhood gun shop, as they will know the details of the law and when and where a CCW course will be given. You will shoot, but you will not learn how to shoot in a CCW class. Rather, you will be given instruction on the law and how it pertains to carrying a firearm.

While there is no federal law specifically addressing the issuance of concealed carry permits, forty-eight states have passed laws allowing citizens to carry certain concealed firearms in public, either without a permit or after obtaining a permit from state or local law enforcement. The states have different terms for licenses or permits. Once you find out the particulars on a CCW class near you, purchase a firearm.

Too often I am asked what kind of pistol I prefer. I never give a clear-cut answer. The make, model and caliber are not as important to me as the user's ability to safely handle a weapon and his ability to discriminate and place effective fire on target.

I would suggest to do a little online research. Visit some credible pistol forums and ask around. You may ask your local gun store clerk, but he or she is no more qualified than anyone else in the world to give you advice on a weapon's purchase.

A pistol should be ergonomically correct for your size and weight and should feel like an extension of your body. It should be comfortable to conceal.

The caliber of the round is not so important as far as terminal ballistics are concerned. A 9 mm round can kill as quickly as a .45 caliber round. That is not an opinion. It is a fact. You may however want to consider what it costs to buy rounds for practice.

You should learn how to use a firearm safely and effectively prior to buying one. Once you have purchased a sidearm, you should obtain a CCW. Firing a pistol effectively is not easy. It requires instruction and practice. In addition, firing a pistol at someone who is threatening you or your principal's life requires compartmentalization and proper mindset.

All weapons training should start with a comprehensive safety briefing. My version of a safety briefing is a bit different than most I have heard on the range. Most versions of this briefing are not thought provoking, and we tend to pay lip service to the standard rhetoric.

I recently took part in a course where the primary instructor gave an abbreviated safety briefing. His reason for brevity was that gun safety was just a matter of common sense. This is true to some degree, but I believe that human beings are capable of momentary lapses of reason.

This is what you may have heard on the range: "Treat every weapon as if loaded." This is the kind of crap you tell your kids so that they will be cautious around guns. Here is another one: "Every gun is always loaded." This is what you tell nonthinkers so that they will treat a weapon like it is a stick of plutonium.

Here is my number one rule of gun handling:

1. Absolutely, positively understand the status of your weapon system at all times!

This is how I brief LEOs and the military. When conducting a status check on your weapon, take steps beyond merely making the requisite motion and sound. One should be cognizant of the status of his weapon before, during, and after the drill or gunfight. Never, ever go into a gunfight with an unloaded gun! If your pistol goes *CLICK* instead of *BANG* in training, you can correct this through immediate action. But a *CLICK* in a gunfight would be a very bad thing.

2. Never cover anything with the muzzle of your weapon that you do not wish to destroy!

If one holds a weapon like it is a weapon instead of a stick of plutonium, he or she will probably be safe. Stay switched on. There are about four conditions a pistol should be in: One is with the magazine out and the slide locked to the rear. Another is in the holster. A third is on target or at a ready position, and the last is in storage. Any other condition may be negligent.

What is important here is that you never stop the gears from turning.

3. Your finger should be off the trigger and the weapon on safe until you have a sight picture and you want the hammer to fall!

This is a never a disabler and can only be an enabler both in training and while on detail. Think of your finger being connected directly to your brain. Any movement off the sights should be followed by your trigger finger moving off the trigger.

4. Identify your target. Know what is behind it, in front of it, and what's flanking it! There is true tactical application in having situation awareness.

If you practice correctly and often, you will be able to access your "hard drive" and subconsciously perform the necessary marksmanship fundamentals while consciously thinking about your principal's safety, overall security concerns, courses of action, fields of fire, and escape routes.

Marksmanship Fundamentals

Sight Alignment & Trigger Control

The two most important fundamentals of marksmanship are *sight alignment* and *trigger control*. All other fundaments are a support mechanism for these two basics. In a gunfight, you can't miss fast enough. The fundamentals need to be rehearsed so that they can be quickly and effectively executed.

The first shot fired is the most important. The first shot fired must be on target. Whether in training or on the two-way firing range, the first shot sets the tempo for all follow-on shots.

Stance

If you encounter a bad thing that intends to inflict harm on you or your principal, you must act swiftly and precisely. In order to ensure shots are on target, you must apply the fundamentals. The fundamentals begin with providing a base to sight alignment and trigger control. This is nothing more than a *semi-athletic stance*. It is your fighting stance. This stance is built into your hard drive's data bank. Your body should be slightly bladed off to the nonfiring side; your weight should be on the balls of your feet, the knees slightly bent; you should also be slightly bent at the waist, and the shoulders should be square to the target.

GRIP

You must next *grip the pistol*. On automatic pistols, there is a *working component* (the slide) and a *stationary component*. Your grip should be as close to the working component as possible. You must also consume as much of the grip with both hands as possible. In addition, your nonfiring, or support hand, should be slightly canted at a forty-five-degree angle to provide more anatomical support to the pistol. You need to firmly support the pistol because you want it to operate on a flat plane so that you can follow up quickly with a series of accurate shots.

PRESENTATION

Next comes your *presentation*. As you press the pistol out to a firing position from a high-ready position, the grip should get tighter. Think of it as physics over strength.

Rely on your brain's default mechanisms and stop making things so complicated. I was told, some years ago, to apply a 70/30 support and strong-hand grip ratio to my pistol. Huh? What if I've got a 60/40? Will I be less effective?

Just grip it steadily enough to control the recoil!

During this presentation, look for your front sight to enter your peripheral vision, and you should start taking the slack out of the trigger. In a perfect world, your sights will be aligned and the hammer will drop as soon as you have reached the apex of your presentation.

Sight alignment is not an option; it's a requirement. The sights built onto your pistol are not a design flaw or a decoration. They are there for a reason. I had a guy today try to sell me on the notion of instinctive fire. Instinctive firing, also called *threat-focused shooting*, is a method of shooting a firearm that relies on a shooter's instinctive reactions, kinematics, and the use of biomechanics that can be used in life-threatening emergencies to quickly engage close targets.

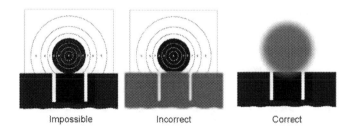

| Impossible | Incorrect | Correct |

It is said that this method of shooting is for use in life-threatening situations where the use of sight shooting cannot be employed due to lack of time to use the gun's sights, low-light conditions, or because of the body's natural reaction to close-quarter threats that prevent meeting the marksmanship requirements of sight shooting. Proponents of this method will tell you that sight alignment is not necessary and that even experienced gun handlers won't look at their sights when firing under duress.

I say bull crap! It is not a disabler to get a sight picture and can only be an enabler.

CONTROL THE TRIGGER

Do not pull, press, or squeeze the trigger. Control requires cognitive thought. Sink your trigger finger as deep as is comfortably possible. Old-school train-of-thought will say "split the last pad." This is old-school. This is an anachronism. This is a *miss* on the target.

Once the hammer falls, it hits the firing pin, which strikes the primer. The shot fires, the gun cycles and chambers the next round. You must next *follow through*.

FOLLOW THROUGH

Follow-through is one of my favorites of all the fundamentals, and it is one of the most neglected. There is no telling how many shots you will need to fire. The fight may take one shot or it may take dumping a magazine into your assailant. You must therefore check your work through your sights. You must do this in training as well. If your drill requires three shots, you must achieve four sight pictures. Not only are you realigning the sights, you are also resetting the trigger. You are now ready to take necessary follow-on shots immediately.

When it comes to marksmanship training, I cannot get enough of the basics. I've run almost four hundred courses to date. The courses ranged from fifteen students to forty. I started every single one of my courses with basic rifle marksmanship (BRM) or basic pistol marksmanship. It did not matter if it was a TAPS (tactical application of practical shooting) course or a hostage rescue course. I still learn something new each time.

Everything starts with a single shot. Marksmanship should be practiced one round at a time. BRM forces us to concentrate on the fundamentals. These fundamentals should be engraved into our hard drives, and we must be able to perform these specific skills intuitively. There are facets that must be felt and performed at a subconscious level—loading, pre-combat check, safety manipulation, building a position, achieving a natural point of aim, sight alignment, trigger control, feeling the metal-on-metal imperfections in the trigger group, calling your shot, seeing how far the sight rises, seeing where the sight settles, following through, realigning the sights, and resetting the trigger. Marksmanship should be practiced in near slow motion.

The more we develop a skill circuit, the less we are aware that we are using it. We are built to make skills automatic, to stash them in our unconscious minds. This process, which is called *automaticity*, exists for powerful, evolutionary reasons. The more processing we do with our unconscious minds, the better our chance for survival.

Fast is fine, but accuracy is final.

—Wyatt Earp

Basic marksmanship allows the shooter to establish a *tempo* or *demeanor*. For comparison's sake, every basketball player in the NBA has a demeanor at the foul line that is unique to him. He goes through the exact drill each time he is at the foul line. He owns it. You should follow a system each time you step to the line.

For example, I would perform a status check of my weapon. I would then check my magazine to ensure that it is loaded. Next, I would insert the magazine all of the way until it locks. I would then charge, press check, seat my bolt with my forward assist, close my dust cover, check my sling, stock, and sight. This, for me, is performed the same way every time.

The greatest percentage of your marksmanship training should revolve around the fundamentals. During these training sessions, it is imperative to self-coach. The most important self-regulatory skill that top performers use during their work is self-observation.

The best performers observe themselves closely. They are able to step outside of themselves and be introspective. They are able to monitor what is happening in their own minds and self-evaluate. This is called *meta-cognition*. Knowledge about your own knowledge or thinking about your own thinking. It's the best way to develop your skills.

Tactical Shooting

Tactical shooting is about *target discrimination* and *proper bullet placement*. It is also about *eliminating predictability*, and *surviving through mobility*. During your shooting drills, always work within your capability level. Make sure that you are hitting what you are aiming at within your limitations and then push those limitations. Encourage yourself to work on accuracy before you try your hand at speed drills. Speed will be a byproduct of working the fundamentals correctly.

TARGET DISCRIMINATION & BULLET PLACEMENT

Being a responsible gun handler means being able to discern and discriminate. Indiscriminate fire is reckless and is for amateurs.

Do not reserve *normal* for yourself. Even in bad neighborhoods, most people are just ordinary people who are trying to live their lives. They may have biases, but they're also just going about their daily lives. Being polite and respectful can get you a long way.

At what point is the threat apparent enough that you should draw your pistol? I guess the situation will have to dictate. With that in mind, practice calling your shot when working accuracy. You should know the location of where your round will impact, good or bad, the second your hammer makes contact with your fining pin. This is called 'calling your shot.'

Next, take a peek at how much your sights rise during recoil and determine whether or not you are controlling recoil. Last, take a look at where your sights settle. They should fall directly back onto the target's center. If they settle off to the left or fight, high or low, you probably have an issue with your natural point of aim. This is going to have an adverse effect on your shot group.

MOBILITY & UNPREDICTABILITY

Remember that during training, you are replicating a possible shooting scenario. In a shooting, someone is typically shooting back at you. This guy has the same brain defaults that you have. You must make a determination when and where to move, and you must do this quickly. At the same time, you must know when to move fast and when to slow down. If you are missing your intended target, slow down. When moving from point A to B, shift into high gear.

Can a twelve-inch lateral move save your life? If you are face to face with a potentially lethal opponent, both of you are thinking about your next action. You are in a virtual chess match where a nanosecond can make the difference between life and death. Brain defaults can force you to make the first move—or to react—based on actions presented to you. The interview stance—which is a neutral, semi-athletic stance in a nonaggressive posture—offers tactical deception. Police officers use this stance when faced with and when questioning an unknown on the streets. You are appearing nonaggressive but are ready for spontaneous, non-telegraphic movement similar to that of a jungle cat!

Police officers work in a profession where deadly uncertainty and terrifying unpredictability are commonplace. They find themselves relying on intuition and split-second decisions to save their own lives and safeguard others. Most decisions, good or bad, are products of training. Many others are hard-drive default mechanism reactions. These defaults are usually correct.

If you find yourself in an interview situation and you determine the person in front of you is likely to act violently, step about a foot to one side and watch the person's reaction. You are going to throw your adversary off track. He or she will be outside of his or her comfort zone because you made a benign movement. Your adversary will become curious and will ask himself, "What does this guy know, and do I want to find out?" This automatically puts you in a physical and tactical advantage while placing your opponent at a mental disadvantage. This will allow you the valuable time you need to execute your plan, and yes you should already have a plan. And it should be one you have rehearsed many times.

Remember, if you are drawing a pistol, it had better be because someone dangerous is directly in front of you and your life or your principal's is being threatened by someone with bad intentions—because this bad guy will be relying on your predictability and his defaults.

So here is my suggestion. Take a short lateral step to the left when performing your tactical draw stroke. It will not slow down your stroke, and it will not throw you off-balance. It will encourage the thought process (your brain works more efficiently when you are moving), and minimize your predictability. It will also temporarily throw off your adversary, which will increase *your* lethality. In a gun fight, temporary is an eternity; being lethal is nonnegotiable.

Why step to the left? Simply because of the law of averages. Ninety-three percent of adult males are right-handed. In addition, most people can't shoot. Most of them will jerk the trigger, which will lead them to hit low and left. Stepping right or left is not the important part. What matters is movement. *Mobility equals survivability.*

We've added movement into our draw stroke to eliminate predictability. We've also increased lethality, which assists in survivability. If you survive, you are a productive part of the team. You are performing the duties of the AIC. You must be decisive and mobile to be lethal and lethal to survive. *Mobility will reduce predictability!*

Hunt It, Kill It, Eat It!

Do not take this literally. It is an idiom of sorts for regaining one's intuitive nature. In each of us lives a primal side, a set of survival skills passed down from a million years ago. It is about pursuing what you want.

Look where you want to go. Don't look where you don't want to go. Whether it's a date with someone you desire or a job opportunity, attitude and intestinal fortitude are necessary ingredients for the stew of life.

Each of us continuously takes in millions of pieces of information every day, the great majority of which are processed unconsciously. Some people take in this information primarily through their five senses—what they see, hear, touch, taste, or smell. Others take in information through their sixth sense, focusing not on what is, but rather on what could be. Each of us has the ability to use both sensing and intuition, and all of us do use both every day.

Intuition is a gift that we humans are born with. We can exercise this function and make it stronger—just like we do with our muscles. Intuition *works* best when we register what we've sensed and then put our five other senses aside. Intuition is our sixth sense, but is often stifled by our over-dependence on the sensations available from the material world. When we tap into our intuition, decisions that seemed difficult to make suddenly gain more clarity.

In our culture, it is easy to lose connection with the fact that we create every single aspect of our existence. Often it may be difficult at the time to see how or why, but we do. Of course, this can be a very hard concept to accept as truth. However, in order to get out of being a victim, it is helpful to just go with this for the moment. So bear with me.

Basically, every step we take toward having complete power over our lives is one step away from being a victim, where we have none. Nowadays, we are so connected, plugged in, that we are disconnected. Our *situational* awareness is nearly nonexistent. We are fat, dumb, and happy button-pushers. Comfortable, flaccid, and complacent.

But being eternally vigilant can be exhausting. Being prepared to save your life or the life of your principals will require work. *Sweat equity.* We expect our kids to look both ways before crossing the street, but we don't want to look behind us while at an ATM. We often relinquish our intuitive nature and do this at great cost to our own safety. Intuitiveness is a gift and a primal instinct that we cannot afford to relinquish. Mitigate having to ask "How did I get here?" A little situational awareness goes a long way.

Try to see things full spectrum. Perform a focal shift in your everyday life. Look around. Slow down before you park and take a look at the other vehicles in your proximity. It is okay. You were born to do this. A successful assault happens with surprise, speed, and violence of action. We can mitigate the surprise by being tuned in or situationally aware. If we take the element of surprise away from a predator, he or she will fear reprisal and forgo the attack.

It is simple tactics. Action versus reaction. If you are aware, you are acting. If you are switched off and have no situational awareness, you are one step behind and will at some point in time fall into a predator's web and be caught reacting.

As mentioned earlier, before you climb out of your vehicle, take a look around and look into the depths. It only takes a second to scan your "primary and secondary sectors." Your *primary sector* is directly outside of your vehicle and your *secondary sector* runs two or three cars deep in all directions. You will see things that you have never seen before. Occasionally, you will find someone looking back at you. Additionally, you will notice how oblivious many people are to their surroundings. This newly acquired awareness will suddenly become a new normal for you.

Get into the habit of backing into a space instead of pulling into it. Not only does this allow for easier departure but may mitigate any would-be scammers looking for you to back into them. Make it routine to hook your keys on a belt loop or clip them onto your purse so they are at the ready. Buy one of those promotional key clips with a built-in light so that you have an emergency light at your disposal at all times.

There are times when you should question intuition. For instance, if it looks good, it may be a diversion.

Diversionary tactics are as old as the day is long—reason being, they are effective. Explosions followed by fireballs and smoke will draw our attention like moth to a flame.

Here is a hypothetical situation: The elevator door opens, you take a step out and something grabs your attention to the right. You get sucked in to staring at this while a predator closes in from the left. Crack to the head . . . lights out. Money and wallet gone.

Next time you are drawn in unexpectedly, take a moment to *look the other way.* Even a snap shot in the other direction can be the determining factor on whether you become a victim or succeed in averting a bad situation. Don't get sucked in by one of the oldest tactics in the book.

Urban Survival Skills

I had a job in Eastern Europe during the Cold War that, in a nutshell, consisted of emplacing spy networks for would-be double agents. It was in a spy hotbed, sort of the epicenter for cat-and-mouse operations. It was 1980s-era high-speed stuff in a low-tech world. Practicing *good demeanor* was a constant mantra. Good demeanor was flavor-of-the-day jargon, so we even had demeanor classes. This cracked me up a bit. When it comes to deportment, you've either got it or you don't. Stevie Wonder could have picked out some Special Ops knuckle-dragger trying to pass as Euro-trash.

In order to blend, one had to walk a line between truly not giving a shit and being completely switched on at the same time.

If you were being sneaky, you stuck out like a rat turd in a sugar bowl. Hiding in plain sight was always the best practice. Be comfortable in your own skin. For instance, if you can't pull off wearing a track suit, mullet, and Bono sunglasses, perhaps donning Bermuda shorts, map in one hand, doner-kebab in the other, with a camera slung around your neck is your best bet in blending in Europe.

There are a lot of guides for kits to help you survive miles from anywhere—but how often do you end up miles from anywhere? What about the everyday, those mundane situations where you constantly find yourself saying, "If only I had . . ." Well, consider putting together an urban survival kit full of the things you need wherever you go. Whenever I fly, I check a bag. This allows me to pack the things I'll need once I land but can't have in the cabin:

Urban Survival Kit

- Pencil and notebook
- Scissors
- Tape
- Pocket knife or multi-tool.
- Lighter
- Flashlight
- Maps
- Other items as needed (see below)

A good pocket flashlight is a must. These days, an LED is the way to go. They're tiny, can be gripped in the mouth for a hands-free job, and they're amazingly bright and long-lasting.

Super glue, duct tape, and para-cord are worth their weight in gold when that certain situation arises where you need an item to make a thing stick to another thing.

Band-Aids, anti-bacterial hand sanitizer, and antibiotic ointment are necessary only when you must leave your room.

The most important part of the urban survival kit never goes inside. In order for these things to be of any use to you, you have to know how to use them. How much good will your cord do you if you can't tie a knot?

Learn to navigate. If the highways are shut down, do you have a surface-street route? If no roads are passable, do you have an off-road route? Practice finding cardinal directions without a compass. If driving is out of the question, do you have a planned walking or riding route? Having maps of your own area is a good idea. Do you have a rendezvous point with other family members?

Survival Tips

Use the word **SURVIVAL** as an acronym to assist you in times when critical thinking is paramount:

> **S**IZE UP THE SITUATION. Take a look around and make sense out of the situation. Look before you leap. Wrap your head around your current situation, internalize it, and do not get into a rush.

> **U**NDUE HASTE MAKES WASTE. If you are rushing, you are not thinking efficiently. Take a bit of time and

make sure you see things as they are the first time around.

➢ **R**EMEMBER WHERE YOU ARE. Maintain a sense of vigilance. Get into a habit of knowing the time, and make mental note of reference points.

➢ **V**ANQUISH FEAR AND PANIC. Use FEAR as an acronym to make it less scary: **F**alse **E**vidence **A**ppearing **R**eal. A little bit of anxiety is a good thing. Being scared shitless weakens one's ability to format thought and perform effectively.

➢ **I**MPROVISE. In order to explore the MacGyver inside of you, it is important to build a basic-skills database.

➢ **V**ALUE LIVING. Depend on yourself to save you. Do not let yourself or your principal down.

➢ **A**CT LIKE THE NATIVES. Do this to a degree. Do not be a poser. Try to pick up moods, demeanors, street habits. Are the inhabitants introverted or extraverted?

➢ **L**EARN THE BASIC SKILLS. Shoot, move, communicate, navigate, medicate, evacuate.

Out with the Family

When traveling with your family, you should follow some basic rules. Follow your instinct. If a person, situation, or location feels wrong or if it makes you nervous, get away as quickly as possible. It is better to walk away, even if it seems overly cautious, than to stay in a situation that might become dangerous.

If you feel as if you are being followed, conduct a surveillance-detection route. Use the same SDR that we discussed in the "Limo Driver" section. Use reflections in vending machines and bus-stop shelters to see behind you. Stop to read a restaurant menu to dissuade a would-be tail. Do not get caught *rubbernecking* if you want to confirm a tail. Turn to look but do not be aggressive of presumptuous. Turning aggressively may not only provoke a thug, but may create one that wasn't there in the first place.

Even in bad neighborhoods, most people are just ordinary people who are trying to live their lives. They may have biases, but they're also just going about their daily lives. Being polite and respectful can get you a long way.

Thugs looking for a victim will typically go after someone who looks timid or lost. Try to appear calm and confident, but do not act like an insider if you're confronted.

Nothing places a bulls-eye on your back in a bad neighborhood like looking lost and confused. If you have the chance, research a neighborhood before you enter it. Look at maps and pictures. Know where you're going and know the surrounding streets well enough to find your way out, if you do get lost, without having to look at a map or ask for directions. Knowing something as simple as, "If I keep heading north on Murray Road, I'll hit Main Street," may be enough. Even if you are lost, pretend you know where you're going.

It is not good enough to "look in both directions" before you cross the street. Get into the habit of looking up and down as well as left and right. Danger can strike from any direction. Don't be naive.

If you're walking toward a person or a group of people who are checking you out, try to walk in a different direction to avoid encountering them. Don't make it obvious. If you cross the street, for example, go into a store on that side so that it seems that's why you crossed. Remember, you want to avoid dangerous situations, but you don't want to come off as paranoid or scared. At the very least, be alert so that you can spot a potential confrontation early enough to cross the street without making it clear to them that you're intimidated.

If you do have to cross paths with shady characters, however, be careful not to quicken your pace (you might do it subconsciously) or make obvious eye contact.

If you are walking with someone, keep your conversation flowing, and avoid topics that might indicate where you are going, where you're from, or what kind of stuff you have.

All of these steps will be harder to follow if you're intoxicated. Going into a bad, unfamiliar neighborhood without your senses fully intact is as street-stupid as it gets.

Stairs, elevators, and parking garages should be avoided altogether if you're getting a bad vibe from the neighborhood.

Do not try to talk like the locals. It is better to be quiet and speak sparingly with your own accent. If you try to use local slang or accent, and you do not pull it off, people might think you're being condescending or downright insulting. At the very least, they may think you are an idiot.

This should be obvious, but definitely do not use any headphone device such as an MP3 player or Bluetooth headset. These items are not only a target for thieves but also critically lessen your awareness of the environment around you, making you an easy target. Likewise, keep cell phone use to a minimum.

Plan your route several days in advance and become familiar with it, also familiarizing yourself with places along it that could be dangerous. Avoid those places. Conduct any business quickly; the less time you have to spend somewhere the better, especially in a bad area. Leave the same way that you came, and make no additional stops that are not absolutely necessary.

Do not become a mark. If you sense that someone is checking you out from afar, let them know that you see them. You can mitigate a surprise attack by simply letting a would-be assailant know that you know.

Always be on the lookout for assets as well as liabilities. Trust your intuition. If a passerby looks like an *asset*—that is, someone who could come to your aid if need be—a nod to say hello now may come in handy when you need him later.

Dress for survival success. Avoid wearing flip flops, high heels, baggy pants, loose bling, head phones, techno-geek gadgets, constricting clothing or being burdened with bags while on your own and especially while with your family! Get off of your phone; don't text while you walk, and pay attention. If you are connected to someone not there, you are disconnected from where you are.

Even if you generally look different from those around you, keeping your clothing understated can go a very long way. This is not the time to look glamorous or unique. See what people your age usually wear in the region and copy them. Do not wear flashy jewelry or bright colors. In some places, certain colors like excessive red or blue are associated with gangs. And, if you are a woman, the most practical advice is *do not look pretty*. Yes, it is a shame that you should have to suppress your individuality, but let's face it, individuality draws attention, and that is not something you want in a dangerous neighborhood.

Familiarize yourself with emergency exits in malls, restaurants, entertainment locations.

What are you carrying on your person? You may consider making it a habit to carry a small flashlight, a blade, and a lighter.

Out of Town

When you check in to a hotel, get two business cards or matchbooks with the hotel name and address on them. Place one by the phone in the room, so you know where you are, and keep the other on you when you leave, so you know where to come back to. If you get lost, you have the address and phone number handy. There is nothing more frustrating than telling a cab driver to take you to the "Marriott" and they ask "which one?" That could be one very expensive cab ride. Or if you are in a country where you don't speak the language, you can simply show a taxi driver the matchbook, and you're on your way back to the hotel.

At night, leave a light on and the drapes partially opened as if someone is inside.

Make your room unattractive to thieves. Give your room the appearance of being occupied. When you leave your room, always leave the television on. Place DO NOT DISTURB sign on the door. If you want maid service, call Housekeeping and tell them to make up the room but leave the sign on the door. The sign is valuable when you aren't in the room, because it gives the impression you are still inside, even if you don't answer the door or the phone.

Know the alternate routes to your room.

Always use the security vault in the hotel. The in-room safe is adequate sometimes. The ones least recommended are those that take standard keys (usually overseas). Preferred are those that have an electronic combination lock. Though more inconvenient, the front desk's deposit boxes are usually safer.

Don't display your guest room key in public or even inside the hotel or at the swimming pool. Crooks have been known to walk by casually, observe the number in the key if stamped on it and make false charges in the hotel restaurant, bar, or store using your room number.

Look for the in-room information about fire safety and read it. Make your family familiar with the nearest fire exit or stairway. Take them on a dry run, walking the stairs until you exit. Find the exit at each end of the hallway. How many doors away? Does the door open easily? Are the exit signs illuminated? Is the stairwell clear of debris? If the lights are out or the way is obstructed, be helpful and contact the front desk to let them know.

Combat Strength Training

Confidence and performance work hand in hand. A comprehensive, functional strength-training program can increase your confidence, because it will change your self-image. The more confidence you have, the more capable you will become.

Trying to talk to a guy about working out is like trying to tell him how to run his barbeque grill. So, if your physical training objectives include chiseled abs and bicep peaks, you should probably skip this chapter.

Fitness training should be a requirement, as it is a necessity when you are a Sentinel and the agent in charge of your protection detail. You do not have the option to dictate your situation, but you can alter the situation's outcome. Ask yourself if you can save your principal's life? Can you hoist yourself over a wall? Can you carry your two children and run full-sprint for fifty meters? Can you kick open the door that is obstructing your getaway? Can you throw that table or chair through the window?

We must understand that we all perform differently and that performance can be measured by doing what you can with what you have. It is important to take care of the combat chassis. Know the status of your body and health.

I train folks in a system that I developed called Combat Strength Training. CST is a system that retrofits the combat chassis so that it performs with maximum efficiency at maximum capacity. Focusing on self-preservation and longevity, CST introduces the chassis and its components to power, strength, and agility training in all planes of motion within the full-muscle-spectrum range. It enhances the chassis' performance and tactical effectiveness through maintenance, education, and combat-replicated movements while following a safe, comprehensive, systematic, and progressive format.

As the chassis is upgraded, it becomes a battlefield multiplier, which in turn becomes a force multiplier. CST improves rate of force production (how much how fast), strength (how much), muscular development, speed, quickness, proprioception—knowing where you are in space—and functional flexibility. The CST methodology works within the individual's own performance level to develop a better, more efficient, stronger, and more capable self.

When it comes to weight training, working body parts is virtually an anachronism. Isolated training of the muscle groups can actually be weakening them, because muscles need to be used in a functional fashion. We should focus on *compound exercises* as they are much more functional than isolated exercises. Changing a tire, lifting a child, moving a table are compound movements. Olympic lifts, for example, are compound exercises.

A chin-up is a compound exercise that, when done with a twist, can elicit a growth response . . . for those of you who want to show off your peaks and valleys. If you are performing fifty *kipping* pull-ups until the skin rips from your hands, you are an idiot. Remember your goal when exercising: to get healthy. Torn hands are not synonymous with health and fitness.

Instead of damaging yourself, add to your *carte du jour* exercises a one-minute chin-up with a long-term goal of being able to achieve three in a row. The concentric movement or upward movement should last 30 seconds, and the eccentric movement or downward movement should last 30 seconds. You will feel at some point other muscles kick in to assist. This is known as *muscle recruitment*. All your muscles understand is applied tension. This exercise offers bang for the buck in muscular endurance and muscular development.

Compound lifts, like Olympic-style lifts, are not only superior for building strength but are also more calorically challenging and elicit greater responses, which generate elevations of testosterone and HGH (human growth hormone). Performing compound lifts like Olympic lifts will result in greater fitness levels, increased caloric expenditure, and improved total body strength and power development. Power cleans, squats, dead-lifts, clean and jerks, are a few examples of Olympic lifts. Changing your exercises on a regular basis and manipulating your volumes and intensity every few weeks will stimulate greater growth and strength.

Before you touch anything that increases resistance, make sure you warm up properly. The purpose is to increase your body temperature to help improve muscle and tendon flexibility and pliability in order to facilitate an improved range of motion.

I am fortunate that I am still in one piece. I spent twenty-two years in the military as a special operations ground pounder and have had several reconstructive surgeries, though at forty-seven, I am fitter than I was at twenty-seven. I did not receive proper strength training instruction until I was thirty-four. This saved me as I was probably on a self-destructive downward spiral.

Here are a couple things I've learned and are testimony to long-lasting performance.

The body needs to be worked in all planes of motion and in the full muscle-action spectrum. In other words, we need to work in the lateral (side to side), sagittal (back and forth), and transverse (core movements) planes of motion. In addition, our combat chassis must produce a variety of actions to effectively manipulate gravity, ground-reaction forces, momentum, and external resistance. Therefore, we must work in the three different actions that the muscles produce: eccentric (lengthening of the muscle), concentric (shortening or contraction), and isometric (equal force or maintaining length).

I am also a firm believer in breaking down the week into sub-tasks. My four-day program includes strength, power, speed/quickness, and muscular development (hypertrophy).

STRENGTH = HOW MUCH

Training example: Max squat, max dead-lift (3 reps each)

Combat application: Up-righting an overturned vehicle, pulling oneself up and over an obstacle

Sentinel application: Holding a dangling loved one by the hand; carrying your principal or principals from point A to point B

POWER = RATE OF FORCE PRODUCTION: HOW MUCH, HOW FAST

Training example: Power cleans, medicine ball throws, lateral sledge hammer throws

Combat application: Hoisting a teammate into a fireman's carry; heaving an ammo can to a top gunner

Sentinel application: Throwing the table through the restaurant window; hoisting an injured loved one into a fireman's carry

SPEED = FAST IN ONE DIRECTION / QUICKNESS = FAST IN MULTIPLE DIRECTIONS

Training example: Sprints, focus—heavy bag work, speed—ladder drills

Combat application: Movement under fire

Sentinel application: Running up a flight of stairs; running through a crowd to the safety of your vehicle; throwing accurate punches in bunches to an adversary's bread basket

Hypertrophy: Muscular Development

Training example: 20 rep sets to failure
Combat application: Self-preservation
Sentinel application: Self-preservation.

In addition to my big four (strength, power, speed/quickness, and muscular development), I will work abs every day, and functional balance and functional flexibility twice a week.

Each workout should be run as a circuit and last 30 minutes or more. Each workout must start with a 5-10 minute warm-up (run a mile, jump rope, row).

Be leery of gimmicky workouts like Cross-Fit. They target a narrow demographic and could do more harm than good. Cross-Fit is a great example of outcome-based training, where one works to a certain time or to a certain number of repetitions instead of concentrating on performance.

Outcome vs. performance. A simple example is Cross-Fit's Workout of the Day (WOD) "Grace": 30 clean and jerks with 135 lbs. for time. This is outcome-based where the exercise becomes subjective. The performance of the exercise becomes secondary to the motion and repetition. An Olympic-style lift should never be timed, in my opinion. What if we were grading our performance instead? I can do a two-minute ten-second Grace. But what am I working? It is not going to make me stronger or better at doing power clean-and-jerks. It is a beat-down. I have risked serious injury for an ego boost. The next time I do it, I will probably score plus or minus ten seconds. Not much of a performance increase. If I wanted to increase my performance at clean-and-jerks, I would seek coaching, increase the weight, work on controlled breathing, reduce the number of breaks, work on mental imagery, etc.

It is not my objective to poo-poo Cross-fit. But besides targeting a narrower demographic than it might, it does not promote self-preservation or longevity. Cross-fit neglects transverse-plane functions, where injury is prevalent especially as we age; it does not work the neck, which supports the *command center*. Cross-fit uses time as a discriminator and often replicates motions daily, leaving little time for recovery. Keep in mind that there is no such thing as over-working, but we can under-recover.

We all have different goals when it comes to our physical training program. For some, it is as simple as cosmetics; for others, it is a requirement. Combat readiness for the Sentinel however, is nonnegotiable. This should be the main focus and should drive what we do and how we do it.

Considering how the human body functions, we must not neglect what is often neglected—grip, neck, and core are the limiting factors to upper-body strength.

One of these limiting factors is grip strength. We are load-bearing creatures. How much we can carry and for how long is usually determined by what our hands can handle. It is one of those neglected and underworked components of our combat chassis.

I trained under the University of Michigan's strength coach Mike Gittleson several times, and he was adamant about working hands to failure. As a matter of fact, he liked to work the entire body to failure. I've also trained with Gym Jones's Mark Twight who disagreed with this to-failure method. I see both sides of the issue and leave it to you.

Working hands in isolation becomes mundane, and we are neglecting the functionality of the exercise. I like to really smoke my hands and forearms at least once a week. I do this with finishing exercises and as a part of a compound movement.

For example, if you did hard pulling work where heavy hand use was part of your routine, you might finish by conducting farmer's walks. As heavy a dumbbell in each hand as possible, walk as far as possible. You will need to conduct these in intervals. Periodically change up the gripping surface of the weight. A small chunk of 4 X 4 or large-diameter bar with the weight suspended below it will require more distal finger strength.

I may go from farmer's walks to rope work. I've got a sixty-foot fast rope that I bring to my gym and use as a finisher. Once exhausted from the workout, I will solicit the assistance of a gym mate. He will wrap the far end around his body and apply manual resistance to the end of the rope. I will assume a modified squatting position and will pull him in. He will resist to the point where I can barely pull him in. Sort of like a one man tug-of-war.

Another area often neglected is our necks. Pencil-neck-itis can land you with a serious injury when an eighteen-wheeler T-bones your limo or when you take a spill down some stairs. The neck supports the *command center*. Simple buddy-assist manual resistance exercises performed twice a week can determine whether you go limp or are able to stay in the fight when taking one on the chin. An example is to have a buddy push you head side to side and back and forth while you are flat on your back with your head extended over the end of a bench press. You supply equal resistance of course.

Another neck exercise I prefer doing is a modified bridge—say on a bench-press bench for example. Less stress on the C-spine and disks than a traditional bridge. Put a towel on the bench, rest your forehead on the towel, set your feet back about a foot or so (the farther back you go with your feet, the more resistance you will add) and perform a series of back-and-forth, up-and-down rotations. The first time you do it, consider starting on your knees instead of your feet. Trust me, if your neck is not used to being worked, and you overwork it, you will be eating through a straw for a couple of days.

For the back of your neck, reverse the process, and for beginners, start on your butt. Take caution. You do not need a lot of resistance. It's your neck we are talking about.

I do not have a specific set of standards when running CST for individuals, particularly because we all perform differently. Some of our combat chassis are Porsches and some of us are Hummers. I would rather the individual set the standard for himself. Training should be comprehensive, systematic, and progressive. I do however encourage an honest look at one's ability to maneuver his body weight. This requires one to be introspective.

I will also encourage individuals participating in my CST program to set ambitious but realistic goals. For example, they should be able to sustain respectable running times in intervals of four hundred meters. They should be able to squat twice their body weight, deadlift twice their body weight, and power clean their body weight.

Hand Combat

The best way to get out of a sticky situation is to never get into it in the first place. One must limit the likelihood of asking, "How did I get here?"

Let's say you got there anyway. What now? Turn and run? What if you are cornered? What if your principal is not capable of running? What if your principal is being harassed? How good do you need to be at fighting? How good do you need to be at self-defense? We can define self-defense as nothing more than recovery from a bad decision or bad luck. You must now be adaptable. I define adaptability as using your existing knowledge to have a positive response to emerging situations.

In your protection detail, your objective is to get out of trouble fast. If your plan goes south, you must fail quickly. You must get back into the mix. Do not let the gears stop engaging. Do not spend any more time than humanly possible lamenting about what and why something you did didn't work. Fail quickly!

Do not get sucked into a fight either. *Set the ego aside and save your hide!* A sociopath might be carrying a straight-edged weapon. You will not know that you are bleeding out until you are passing out.

As often as I get asked to recommend a handgun, I get asked what I believe to be the most effective fighting style. Uh, I'm not sure that there is one. A sociopath with zero training in martial arts can probably tear the walls down on a black belt with no chutzpah. Cunning, strategy, tactical deception, and audacity will win the day over how well you can punch the air or break a board.

Professional fighters are extremely devoted. Most are born with athleticism and dedicate years to their craft. Even a professional fighter will default back to primal skills and lose style points in a street fight, where there is no information about your opponent, no specific start time, no set venue, and no rules!

Styles are numerous. Most fighters and fans of fighting are passionate about a certain style. For instance, *jiu-jitsu* proponents will tell you that 95 percent of all street fights end on the ground, so ground fighting should be studied as your primary means of self-defense. I agree that jiu-jitsu is an effective style of fighting, especially while it teaches that a smaller, weaker person can successfully defend against a bigger, stronger assailant by using leverage and proper technique—most notably by applying joint locks and chokeholds to defeat the other person. However, approximately 100 percent of fights start on one's feet. If you intentionally take matters to the ground, you are relinquishing your number-one defense mechanism as a human being, which is mobility . . . and . . . ? You got it, *mobility equals survivability.*

Decades ago, I dabbled in Taekwondo, which is a Korean martial art and the national sport of South Korea. I then moved on to Muay Thai while working in Thailand. Muay Thai is a combat sport from Thailand that uses stand-up striking along with various clinching techniques. This vicious closed-quarter style of fighting sold me when I got my ass handed to me by a 140-pound Asian guy. Years later, I got my ass handed to me again, but this time in a boxing ring.

Just when I thought I was invincible, I got dropped by a left hook. Back to the basics I went.

Since this is an emotional topic, I will preface this next bit by stating that this is my opinion. I am just one guy with lots of opinions, and here is one of them:

If you want true bang for the buck, join a boxing gym. Boxing skills will build a sound foundation on which all other styles of fighting can set. Lateral movement, non-telegraphic motion, zone awareness, spontaneity, and fear management are all skills you can learn from boxing. You will learn quickly how to throw straight and accurate punches in bunches with devastating effect.

We are not all born with rhythm and athleticism, and those are things that cannot be taught. You can, however, learn to manage and compartmentalize your anxiety. You can become aware of your safety—or reactionary—zone. You can also learn how to take a punch and how to throw an effective blow without broadcasting it. These can all be learned fairly quickly when being taught by an experienced boxing coach.

If you learn and practice the most basic of boxing moves, you will know more than most of the thugs on the street. These moves work well from a nonaggressive stance. Being nonaggressive is of huge tactical importance. You can either escalate aggressive behavior or deescalate it depending on your demeanor. You want to change the tempo of the aggressive behavior to act in your favor. You may even win the day through psychological operations and tactical deception. Psychological operations are planned operations to convey selected information to influence emotions, motives, and objective reasoning

There are plenty who will argue that I am dead wrong. Understandable! Fighting and styles is an emotional topic. At the end of the day, it doesn't matter. If we are attacked with surprise and violence of action, no amount of training can save us. We can mitigate the surprise by exercising a little situational awareness.

This is worth mentioning again. If we take the element of surprise away from a predator, he or she will fear reprisal and forgo the attack.

It is simple tactics. Action versus reaction. If you are aware, you are acting. If you are switched off and have no situational awareness, you are one step behind and will at some point in time, fall into a predator's web.

In "Shooting 101," we discussed the lateral move. If you are face to face with a potentially lethal opponent or a sociopath, both of you are thinking about your next act. You are in a physical chess match where a nanosecond or an inch can make the difference between life and death.

Keep your hands up in front of you, as you would when talking with your hands. You are keeping your hands and arms between you and your opponent. You are appearing nonaggressive but are ready for spontaneous, nontelegraphic movement.

Do not allow your opponent to enter your safety zone. You have become more aware of this zone at your boxing gym though *controlled sparring*.

At some point, when the aggression level of your adversary escalates, you must make an obvious lateral move. This simple one-step lateral move to the left or to the right will throw your opponent off track. As stated previously, your adversary will become curious. He or she will ask himself, "What does this guy know, and do I want to find out what he knows?" This automatically puts you in a physical and tactical advantage while placing him or her at a mental disadvantage. You got inside of your adversary's *OODA loop!*

The **OODA loop** (for *observe, orient, decide, and act*) is a concept originally applied to the combat operations process, often at the strategic level in military operations. It is now also often applied to understanding commercial operations and learning processes. The concept was developed by military strategist and USAF Colonel John Boyd.

A predator on the street is like a predator in the wild. The predator in the wild must not become injured. If injured in the wild, it will lose its ability to hunt; it will starve and die. A predator on the street is no different. If he or she feels threatened, he or she will think twice about attacking.

If your adversary enters your zone after you have made several attempts to defuse any physical confrontation, you must strike first. Your boxing skills will enable you to throw a fast, straight, range-finding *number one*—a *jab*—followed by a devastating *number two*—a *cross*. A sucker punch and a follow-up. You have mitigated looping telegraphic punches. The combination is followed by an additional lateral move and a recock. Your point of aim is center-mass fleshy nose. When the jab strikes the nose, the eyes water and the adversary shuts down for a nanosecond, allowing proper placement of the number two, or cross, which is a commitment, but a devastating commitment.

First Aid

The Sentinel must be familiar and current with basic lifesaving procedures. It is not a scenario you want to imagine, but you must be prepared to render first aid to your principal. An injury may look more severe than it really is. Head cuts, for instance, bleed a lot! Stay calm. The human body is resilient. It may not be as bad as it appears.

What is the first thing to do when you find your principal unconscious? You should probably conduct a primary survey. The acronym to help you remember the primary survey steps is DRAB: Danger, Response, Airway, Breathing. After that, it's as easy as ABC: Airway, Breathing, Circulation.

DANGER

Are you or the casualty in any danger? If you have not already done so, make the situation safe and then assess the casualty.

RESPONSE

If the casualty appears unconscious, check this by shouting, *"Can you hear me?" and "Open your eyes!"* and gently shaking his or her shoulders.

If there is a **response and** no further danger, leave the casualty in the position found and summon help if needed.

- Treat any condition found and monitor vital signs—level of response, pulse, and breathing.

- Continue monitoring the casualty either until help arrives or he or she recovers.

If there is *no* **response**:

- Shout for **help.**
- If possible, leave the casualty in the position found and open the airway.
- If this is not possible, turn the casualty onto his or her back and open the airway.

Airway

- Open the airway by placing one hand on the casualty's forehead and gently tilting the head back.
- Lift the chin using two fingers only.
- This will move the casualty's tongue away from the back of the mouth.

Breathing

- Look, listen, and feel for **no more** than 10 seconds to see if the casualty is breathing normally.
- Look to see if the chest is rising and falling. Listen for breathing.
- Feel for breath against your cheek.
- Check for other life-threatening conditions such as severe bleeding and treat as necessary.
- If the casualty is **not breathing normally,** or if you have any doubt whether breathing is normal, begin CPR.

As a first-aider, the priorities when dealing with a casualty are always the same:

Airway
Breathing
Circulation

A primary survey (DRAB) of a casualty will help you to establish priorities within those ABCs.

A primary survey allows you to get your head in the game. It will assist you in sizing up the situation and assessing the severity of the injury, thus mitigating jumping to conclusions.

When dealing with an unconscious casualty you should *open and maintain their airway* as your first priority. If the airway should become obstructed, possibly by the tongue falling to the back of the throat, then the casualty will be unable to breathe, and this will lead to death if untreated.

If the casualty is breathing, the simple procedure of placing the casualty into the recovery position should ensure that the airway will remain clear of obstructions. All forms of the recovery position share basic principles. The patient is on his side, the mouth is downward so that fluid can drain from the patient's airway; the chin is well up to keep the epiglottis opened. Arms and legs are locked so as to stabilize the position of the patient

If the casualty has stopped breathing, you can assist him or her by performing a combination of chest compressions and rescue breaths. You breathe out enough oxygen to potentially keep the casualty alive until the emergency services arrive; the oxygen you breathe into the casualty will need to then be pumped around the body using chest compressions.

It is important to remember that in any life-threatening situation the emergency services (911 in North America, 999 in the UK) should be called as soon as breathing or absence of breathing has been identified.

Check the victim for unresponsiveness. If the person is not responsive and not breathing or not breathing normally. Call 911 and return to the victim. In most locations, the emergency dispatcher can assist you with CPR instructions.

If the victim is still not breathing normally, coughing, or moving, begin chest compressions.

- Push down in the center of the chest two inches 30 times. Pump hard and fast at the rate of at least 100/minute, faster than once per second.
- Tilt the head back and lift the chin.
- Pinch nose and cover the mouth with yours and blow until you see the chest rise. Give 2 breaths. Each breath should take 1 second.
- CONTINUE WITH 30 PUMPS AND 2 BREATHS UNTIL HELP ARRIVES.

CPR procedures change often. Recently, popular school of thought deletes the need to rescue breathe and uses compressions alone. Check with an EMT for the latest and greatest CPR procedures.

Your Med Bag

As the lead to your protection detail, you must be prepared at all times. I have three complete first-aid kits. One is in a central location in my house. One of them travels with me while on duty with my principal, and the last one is in my Tough Box or Go Box. We will discuss the purpose and contents of the Go Box a little later. Is it overkill? Beats me, but I do know that it is better to have and not need than to need and not have. Here are some things to consider as contents to your first-aid kit:

- 1 roll of absorbent cotton
- Syrup of ipecac to induce vomiting
- Antihistamine for allergic reactions
- Iodine antiseptic solution
- Aspirin (for adult use only) and acetaminophen and ibuprofen (in child and adult dosages)
- One-inch-wide adhesive tape
- Bacitracin ointment to treat cuts, scrapes, or puncture wounds
- Bandages in various sizes
- Butterfly bandages and thin adhesive strips (Steri-strips)to hold skin edges together
- Calamine lotion
- Cold pack
- Mouthpiece for protection when performing mouth-to-mouth resuscitation (or a dental dam with a hole cut out)
- Cotton-tipped swabs
- Elastic bandage or wrap

- Eyedropper for irrigating
- Flashlight
- Four-inch x four-inch gauze pads
- Disposable surgical gloves
- Matches
- Saline eye drops
- Scissors
- Safety pins
- Sewing needle to help remove a splinter
- Thermometer
- 2 triangular pieces of cloth to use as slings or to cut up as bandages or straps
- Tweezers

Your House, Your Fortress

In your fortress, you are not just protecting yourself and your principal from burglars, but also from natural disasters, power outages, and fire.

According to FBI statistics, a house, apartment, or condominium is burglarized once every fifteen seconds. Fortunately, burglary is probably the most preventable of crimes. By taking a few simple precautions, you can dramatically reduce the risks.

Of course, every home and every situation is different, and there are no guarantees.

The first step is to determine what kind of threat you are trying to protect against. For example, defending against personal threats, such as assault, requires different measures than defending against burglary.

Most home burglars do not give great amounts of thought to planning the job and assessing the benefits vs. dangers, but understanding how they choose a target can go a long way in reducing your chances of being a victim.

Most burglars look for:

- Something worth stealing
- Easy access combined with low visibility
- A home that is unoccupied

Rule number one: Make your home less attractive to rob than your neighbor's. My home is lit up at night. Every bit of dead space is decoratively and defensively illuminated.

Rule number two: Do not invite your house to be cased. If you have stuff worth stealing, limit the number of people you tell. It may be unintentional, but people talk and word travels.

Rule number three: Get a dog. A dog is one of the best deterrents. Not because it's vicious—it need not even be seen—but it has to be heard. A dog with a menacing bark will scare away a lot of would-be burglars, not only because they don't know what kind of dog you have and what risk it would be to them if try tried to break in, but more likely because a noisy dog will create a disturbance and get attention—the last thing a burglar wants!

You should take a walk around and through your property often. Start outside and ask yourself, *How would I best break in?* I do this at night as well.

Besides an obvious lived-in look, don't get into a habit of doing certain things only when you're not home, whether it's pulling the drapes, putting on the lights, or coiling up the hose. Chances are good you can tell when your neighbor isn't home. Remember it's a burglar's job to know the same things. Most professional criminals can tell nobody's home at least four or five houses away.

Several dead giveaways are closing the drapes *only* when you're not home. Having no garbage cans out on collection day or an empty can sitting at the curb are tip-offs you're not home. So are closing up the house as tight as a drum in the hot summer months without the air-conditioner running. Turning on a certain light or two and every other room is in total darkness. Ditto for picking up all the kid's toys, taking in the dog, shutting the garage door if you frequently leave it open, and turning off the lawn sprinkler.

Install lights to cover dead space. Electronic devices that are effective, besides the typical whole-house alarm systems for windows and doors, are infrared or motion detectors that sense heat given off by one's body or movement. Anyone approaching too close will trigger any number of attached devices. The most effective are powerful lights or burglar horns that either flood the area with light or fill the air with a deafening sound without notice. Just like a barking dog, the would-be burglar will usually hightail it out of there for fear of being discovered.

To be effective, the sensitivity of such devices much not be set too high, otherwise stray animals will set them off too frequently, which will get you on the wrong side of your neighbors. Also be sure such devices are high enough off the ground that they can't be easily turned off or broken.

Illegal entry right through the front door occurs more often than all other points of entry combined! All exterior doors should be of solid hardwood or steel-reinforced. A good door does no good if the door frame is in bad shape or of inferior construction. Pay special attention to the door jambs. Most, even in expensive homes, are made out of cheap pine. It doesn't take much force to kick in the door even if it's protected with deadbolts, if the strike plate is attached with only a couple of half-inch or three-quarter-inch screws.

Take a few minutes and install two-and-a-half to three-inch stainless steel or nickel-plated screws in all your exterior door jambs. Be sure screws go at least one and three-quarter inches deep into the underlying framing lumber. While you are at it, consider getting heavy-duty strike plates or a door reinforcement kit sold in many larger home improvement centers. Be advised you may have to chisel out more of the door jamb to install it, but it's worth the effort for the greater protection provided. Another way to increase the chances of your door holding is to further protect it from being kicked in by installing a device on the floor inside center that the door rests against when shut and swings away when the door opens. This device can be as simple as a rod cut to fit the rail well of the closed door and set in the well.

Since sliding doors are a favorite target, install several screws into the door's upper track to guard against it being lifted up and out of its track. Open and shut the door through its entire range to allow just enough of the screw's head protruding to allow free movement without allowing the door to be removed. Several devices can be installed into the door's upper or lower track that act much like a dead bolt by running a heavy pin through the door track and deep into the frame. Just having a length of old broom handle set in the door's lower track also prevents the door from easily being forced open and works nearly as well.

Your garage door is easy pickings unless you have an electronic door opener. Today these devices are fairly cheap (around $150 USD) and make it practically impossible to force open the overhead door from the outside without breaking through the actual door panels, because of the high tension produced from the worm drive or chain device that makes the opener work. Yes, it is possible for a burglar to punch in the right code and gain access, but with today's remote controls providing so many possible combinations, the odds are very slight, and the burglar won't waste the time trying all the possibilities.

Burglars break windows as a last resort—or by accident. The preferred method is cutting an access hole or slipping in a thin stiff wire and undoing the locking device. Most double-hung windows have cheap locks that should be replaced by heavy-duty sash locks or even keyed locks, if you can put up with the inconvenience. An old trick is installing a small eyebolt in either corner. If done correctly, the window can't be opened from the outside with the eyebolt in place.

If you find yourself in a position where you are considering using deadly force, identify your target as "friend or foe" before you fire. We've all heard the stories about someone shooting a "burglar" in the dark only to find out it's a family member. *Make sure of your target.* You might consider a high-quality small flashlight like the ones made by <u>Surefire</u> brand. But don't get sucked into a fight.

Don't go looking for trouble. If at all possible, don't go downstairs or into the front of the house to investigate an unusual noise. Most homes offer a hallway to the bedrooms that's easily defended versus having to cover all the hiding places in your living room, den, kitchen (with all those knives), and so on. Besides which, you've probably just woken up—your eyes are bleary or maybe you have a tendency to cough or sniffle when you've been disturbed in the night. In any case, getting up and moving about will probably alert any intruder of your whereabouts before you know about theirs.

Instead, move family to a safe room. If you have children, you may elect to move them to the room that is your safest room of the house. This is usually the master bedroom—where you have your firearm, a telephone, and a last-ditch escape route out of the house. Remember the risk of trying to move elderly relatives and small children who may cry upon sudden awakening.

Call police as soon as possible. If possible, have your spouse or another family member call the police as soon as you can. Ideally this will be after you have secured everyone in one safe room of the house. Depending on your circumstances, you might consider keeping a cell phone in the bedroom. If your phone lines have been cut (which is common if you appear to have an alarm system), you'll still be able to summon help.

Be sure your family is behind you and out of the line of fire. If you moved everyone to a safe room, you should be closest to the door, so you have a clear line of fire. If you can't move everyone into one room, you may have to take a position in a hallway where they remain *behind* you. The last thing you want is to be squeezing the trigger on the shithead at the end of the hallway when your child sleepily steps into the hallway!

Never block an intruder's escape route. If you can avoid it, never put yourself between an intruder and his most likely exit. Doing so can put you in danger if he's surprised and bolts for the exit toward you. It's better to let home invaders flee than find out they are faster, stronger, or more determined than you are.

If your intruder discovers that you are awake or present and shows himself to you, in a firm voice—as firm and controlled as you can muster at the moment—give him the command, "Don't Move!" Assuming you see no weapons in his hands, follow this *immediately* with the command, "Get face down on the ground, now!" If the person turns and flees, fine and dandy; don't give chase; let the cops do that.

If the intruder stays put, however, and refuses your commands, *watch his or her hands carefully*. If you feel the situation cannot be controlled verbally or if the intruder makes any movement toward you, armed or not, he or she isn't being deterred by your firearm and is an *immediate threat* to your safety! It is a time to act. This is a key point:

watch his or her <u>hands</u>! If you can't see both hands, you don't know if he or she has a weapon! If you can see that the intruder is armed with a knife or gun, use your best judgment. But remember to put your front sight on your target. At most household ranges, elevation doesn't matter too much; if you see the front sight sticking up in the middle, that's probably close enough. Shoot to kill. You should cease firing when the person stops being a threat.

Regardless of whether the intruder has fled, been wounded, or been killed, be sure to wait for the police to come check the house to be sure he—*or his companion you didn't know about*—is not hiding somewhere. If you hear or see him fleeing outside, turn on all lights, including exterior lights until the police arrive, but always be alert for a second, unseen intruder!

For those who think they are tough-guys, remember that you will have just awakened. Perhaps your eyesight will be blurry, or you cough after standing up. Perhaps you'll find your arm is totally asleep and as useful as an anchor. Intruders have the advantage in most cases; they're dressed, pumped on drugs or adrenaline, their eyes are used to the dark, and they may be armed. No matter how tough you think you are, your voice may crack like an adolescent's, your hands will shake, and your heart will be pounding in your ears. Don't ever count on being ready! Think ahead!

Safe Haven

Identify a safe-haven room in your house and ensure your family is briefed and practiced on its usage. A room in the residence in the inner perimeter of security is the safe-haven room. It doesn't have to be a hidden fortress room like the panic rooms in the movies, but it should be suitable as a temporary refuge to the principals when additional time is needed for police or security personnel to respond to the residence under attack. When identifying a room in the residence as a safe haven, the following factors should be considered.

Accessibility

The principal should not be exposed to additional danger while moving to the safe haven. If possible, this room should be the master bedroom.

Ability to Secure

This applies to both the safe haven and its route.

Ability to Defend

The safe haven should be within an established realistic perimeter that the protection detail (you) can defend. It also should have a tactical advantage (i.e., high ground).

ABILITY TO COMMUNICATE

The command post or headquarters must be accessible. In order to alert local police, one should have a reliable landline and cell phone close at hand.

ABILITY TO ESCAPE

If perimeter rings are compromised, there must be an escape route.

ABILITY TO HOLD

With appropriate equipment and supplies, the safe haven should be able to hold for fifteen to sixty minutes while under siege. The safe haven is considered to be the core of the inner perimeter ring.

Protecting the HQ

You and your principal should be most secure when in your residence. There, the protection detail (you) has the greatest opportunity to control the environment. This is accomplished through the use of concentric security rings, physical security hardware, electronic alarms, and a general familiarity with the area surrounding the residence.

It is good practice to dry run your residence as if an invader has breached your perimeter. Now you must conduct close-quarter battle (CQB) to eliminate the threat.

CQB is defined as a short-duration, high-intensity conflict, characterized by sudden violence at close range.

In the typical CQB scenario, the attackers try a very fast, violent takeover of a vehicle or structure controlled by the defenders (you), who usually have no easy way to withdraw. Because enemies, loved ones, and other principals can be closely intermingled, CQB demands a rapid assault and a precise application of lethal force. The Sentinel needs great proficiency with his weapons, but also the ability to make split-second decisions in order to avoid or limit *friendly* casualties—that's when you make a mistake and someone in your family gets hurt because of it.

You do not have to be an expert at CQB, but you do need to follow simple rules:

Do not get sucked into the fight.

Call the police for help as soon as you can. It is one thing to be able to hit a target on a flat range and a completely different experience to hit a target who has a beating heart, is moving, is in the dark, has evil intent, and is scaring the crap out of you.

You must also discern, discriminate, move, and seek cover while your adversary is doing the same.

If you have a weapon at home for protection, it is useless without ammunition. Have magazines loaded. In a crisis situation, you will probably not have time to load magazines. When you go investigate a bump in the night, you have to be ready for a violent confrontation. Keep your weapon in a place where you can get to it and load it in the dark.

Keep a small flashlight with your pistol as well.

Even better, a pistol with a gun light mounted on it becomes a battlefield multiplier. Understand its status. You do not want to go into a gunfight with an unloaded gun.

If you make the determination to investigate, use *defilade*. You are in "in defilade" if you use natural or artificial obstacles to shield or conceal yourself to mask your position. You should also pie off adjoining rooms. This is sometimes called *slicing the pie*—the goal of this angular search is to spot the enemy without him spotting you. Clear as much of a room from the adjoining room before moving on. Avoid being backlit or silhouetted in door openings. You will make yourself an easy target. Dry runs will mitigate this error.

Use limited visibility as a battlefield multiplier. You know your area of operation better than the piece of crap who has just invaded it. If you turn on the lights, you are no longer on equal footing. You have the tactical advantage in your home in the dark.

Use your light when you need it *only*!
Do not lead with your face!

Clear corners or enter rooms from a crouch. People are preprogrammed to pick up patterns of predictability (fun to say). Entering low will make you a smaller target, help to eliminate predictability, and give you a higher takeoff angle on your shots fired, which will reduce *collateral damage*—a term that has no mitigation if it occurs in your home with your family.

Stay as close to the walls as possible to give yourself a greater perspective on the entire room. If you are entering a room to the middle, you must clear 360 degrees of it.

Disaster Preparation

The idea behind natural disaster preparation is to *be prepared* for utility loss, service loss, mobility loss, convenience loss, or for bad people looking to take advantage of others. Residents of remote areas should already know that restoration will take longer for them; therefore, some checklist items, like food, require a larger reserve inventory than in central or high-density areas.

Being prepared can reduce fear, anxiety, and additional losses that accompany disasters. Communities, families, and individuals should know what to do and where to seek shelter in the event of a fire, hurricane, flood, earthquake, civil unrest, and tornado. They should be ready to evacuate their homes and take refuge in public shelters and know how to care for their basic medical needs.

Specific types of disasters will require specific types of active preparation. For example, in an area known for flooding, one should consider having a one-way sewage valve that prevents sewage from reversing direction when the water treatment facility has a higher water/flood level than a residence. In earthquake areas, homes must have a gas shutoff valve to help prevent dangers from gas leaks. The Red Cross and some government agencies have further details about specific natural disaster readiness. Be sure to check your local recommendations.

Remember, we do not plan to fail; we fail to plan. Sometimes it is better to have and not need than to need and not have.

After a major disaster, the usual services we take for granted, such as potable running water, electricity, refrigeration, and telephones, may be unavailable. Experts recommend that you should be prepared to be self-sufficient for at least three days. Store your household disaster kit in an easily accessible and well-protected location. Put contents in a large, watertight container (e.g., a large plastic garbage can with a lid and wheels) that you can move easily.

Your basic emergency kit should include:

Water—one gallon per person per day
Food—ready to eat or requiring minimal water
Manual can opener and other cooking supplies
Plates, utensils and other feeding supplies
First-aid kit and instructions
A copy of important documents & phone numbers
Warm clothes and rain gear for each family member.
Heavy work gloves
Disposable camera
Unscented liquid household bleach and an eyedropper for water purification
Personal hygiene items including toilet paper, feminine supplies, hand sanitizer, and soap
Plastic sheeting, duct tape, and utility knife for covering broken windows
Tools such as a crowbar, hammer & nails, staple gun, adjustable wrench, and bungee cords.
Blanket or sleeping bag

Large heavy-duty plastic bags and a plastic bucket for
waste and sanitation
Any special-needs items for children, seniors or people
with disabilities. Don't forget water and supplies
for your pets.

Having a gasoline-operated power generator may
prove to be a worthy investment. If you own one, store it in
a location where you do not have to move it to operate it.
Keep extension cords with it. Start it up once a month and
let it run. Store five gallons of gas with it.

Most average homes of 1,200 to 3,000 sq. ft. can run
critical items in the home by using a 5,000-7,000-watt
generator. The most common items that need emergency
power during a blackout would be the furnace blower
motor, refrigerator, freezer, lights, TV, sump pump, and
water pumps. Larger standby generator systems in the
10kW-12kW range will quietly supply as much as 15,000
watts of starting power to your home, automatically giving
your family the power, freedom and comfort of their usual
lifestyle, uninterrupted by power failure.

But to know for sure what your needs are, you should
have a *load analysis* done by a qualified electrician or
generator vendor. Most vendors will perform this for you
free of charge, and that will help you determine exactly
which size generator you need.

Communication

One of the first things that will fail in a disaster is electronic communications. Unfortunately, it is one thing we need most following a disaster. Most families are separated during the day and sometimes the evening. With parents working, kids going to school and their after school activities, we are rarely together at all times.

We already know how important it is to have emergency supplies on hand. Besides your all-encompassing home kit, you should have smaller emergency kits that can be picked up and are always ready to grab and go. Emergency food and water are a must.

If disaster strikes though, how will you be able to communicate with your spouse or child if their phones are down? Establish a family disaster-preparedness communication plan.

I found this acronym on a FEMA website:

Create a family communication plan so that you can get in touch with family members. Give copies of contact information and meeting locations to everyone in your family

Options are available: telephones, cell phones and e-mail are all great ways to get in touch with family members.

Make sure you know the emergency plan at your child's school.

Make a decision about where you will meet in case you can't get home during an emergency.

Understand that it may take time to get through to everyone. Try to be patient.

Needs of your pets should be kept in mind. Keep a pet carrier for easy transport.

Inform yourself. Watch news broadcasts, read online news updates, or listen to a battery-operated radio for official guidance during an emergency, but also prepare in advance.

Copies of your emergency plan should be in your emergency supply kit in case you need to leave in a hurry.

Ask kids to discuss their concerns and feelings. Do they understand the family plan?

Take the kids to visit the *meeting spots* so that they are familiar and feel comfortable finding them on their own if necessary.

Emergencies take many forms. Categorize different types of emergencies and discuss the level of concern related to each and how that is reflected in your family plan.

"Have a plan" is one of the first things every preparedness guide out there tells you to do . . . yet almost none of them offer much assistance with how to develop the plan. One of the many acronyms used by the military, PACE, can assist you in making a Plan B for the sudden emergency event:

Primary
Alternate
Contingency
Emergency

The military teaches this acronym for tactical-communications planning and, when followed, works quite well. This level of planning can be used for day-to-day communications and easily fits into a deteriorating *SHTF* situation—when you-know-what hits the fan—just as well.

- **P** = The *primary* and routine method of execution for whatever is happening. For normal day-to-day operation, this might mean cell-phone communication. Most all of us use these and under *normal* conditions, they work as expected. The agreement is this: "I will call you when I arrive at _____."
- **A** = The *alternate* method of accomplishing the task with minimal to no other impact. In this example, a landline would be a suitable alternate to a cell phone. The sacrifice made by using the landline is the minor inconvenience of having to stop en route and find a pay phone or borrow a local line from someone. The alternate method should not be overly burdensome—it is supposed to have similar *cost* to the primary method, but just be another way of accomplishing the task. Ideally, the first two methods could be swapped back and forth with little to no impact. The agreement is this: "When I arrive at _____, if the cell phone doesn't work, then I will call you from a landline."
- **C** = The *contingency* method of accomplishing the task kicks in when things start getting difficult. This method will not be as fast, easy, or convenient as the first two methods but it is capable of accomplishing the task in an acceptable time frame. To continue this example, a portable HAM

radio or walkie-talkies could be considered a suitable device Perhaps a third-party is brought in, a neighbor, an office mate, someone who might be able to pass a message. This person should be made aware he or she is part of your emergency contingency plan. The agreement is this: "When I _____, then I will _____." I am not suggesting that we should carry walkie talkies in our bags.

E = Then there are the *emergency* methods of accomplishing the task. This method is the method of last resort and typically has significant delays or impacts to the overall timeline. To complete this example, a human courier carrying a handwritten message could be an emergency means of communication.

Be Prepared to Bug Out

It is your job as the Sentinel to ask "What if?" Come up with as many scenarios as possible from best- to worst-case scenarios and ask yourself if you can handle it.

When I think worst case, one thing that crosses my mind is a catastrophic event, a natural devastating disaster, or mass civil disobedience—a scenario where I've got to get out of Dodge in a hurry. I wonder what it would be like to have just minutes to pack my family into my Suburban and hit the gas.

Since I will have to plan on the fly, I have already packed for this event that I hope never comes. I have a *bug-out bag* in my garage, ready to be loaded up. The primary purpose of a bug-out bag is to allow you to evacuate quickly if a disaster, civil disobedience, or other catastrophic event should occur.

It is prudent to gather all of the materials and supplies that might be required to do this into a single place, such as a bag, box, or a few storage containers. Your household disaster kit doubles as your three-day bug-out bag. I've got mine in a single large Tough-Box that I picked up from Lowes.

It is recommended that a bug-out bag should contain enough supplies for seventy-two hours. This advice comes from organizations responsible for disaster relief and management in that it may take them up to seventy-two hours to reach people affected by a disaster.

The bag's contents may vary according to the region of the user, whereas someone evacuating from the path of a hurricane might need different supplies from someone who lives in an area prone to tornadoes or wildfires.

In addition to allowing one to survive a disaster evacuation, a bug-out bag may also be utilized when sheltering in place as a response to emergencies such as house fires, blackouts, tornadoes, civil unrest, and other severe natural disasters.

The suggested contents of a bug-out bag vary, but most of the following are usually included:

Enough food and water to last for seventy-two hours.

Water for washing, drinking, and cooking. US recommends 1 gallon (3.78 liters) per person per day. Be sure to include your pets in the count.

A first-aid kit

Fire-starting tool (matches, lighter, sparker)

Nonperishable food

Water-purification supplies

Standard camping equipment, including sanitation supplies, cooking, and eating supplies

A disaster plan including location of emergency centers, rallying points, possible evacuation routes etc.

GPS

Professional emergency literature explaining what to do in various types of disaster. You will have studied and understood this material before the actual disaster, but you should keep it here for reference in the event.

Maps and travel information

Weather-appropriate clothing (e.g., poncho, headwear, gloves, etc.)

Bedding items such as sleeping bags and blankets

Enough medicine to last an extended evacuation period

Medical and financial records

Pet, child, and elderly care needs

Battery- or crank-operated radio

Lighting (battery- or crank-operated flashlight, glow sticks)

Firearms and appropriate ammunition

Cash and change, as electronic banking transactions may not be available during the initial period following an emergency or evacuation

Positive Identification, such as driver's license, state ID card, or social security card

Fixed-blade and folding knife

Duct tape and rope/paracord

Plastic tarps for shelter and water collection

Slingshot, pellet gun, blowgun or other small-game hunting equipment

Wire for binding and animal traps

Go Bags

A go bag is something that travels with you all the time. It is a bug-out bag in miniature. It contains some of the same items that the bug-out bag would but in smaller format. Keep it in the trunk of your car.

Put the following items together in a backpack or another easy-to-carry container in case you must evacuate your vehicle quickly:

Batteries
Radio—battery operated
Whistle
Spare cell phone battery
Dust mask
Pocket knife
Matches, lighter, or fire-starting kit
Suspension cord (para cord)
Emergency cash in small denominations and quarters for phone calls
Sturdy shoes, a change of clothes, and a warm hat
Local map
Some water and food
Permanent marker, paper, and tape
Photos of family members and pets for identification purposes
List of emergency point-of-contact phone numbers

List of allergies to any drug (especially antibiotics) or
food
Copy of health insurance and identification cards
Extra prescription eyeglasses, hearing aid, or other vital
personal items
Prescription medications and first-aid supplies
Extra keys to your house and vehicle

The 7 Ps

Proper planning and preparation prevents piss-poor performance. This adage is normally referred to as *the 7 Ps* rather than as an acronym. PPPPPPP just doesn't cut it in any circles. Educators and trainers in military and civilian situations find it useful to introduce it as "the 7 Ps" before explaining it. The humor and shock of the mild expletive help make the caution memorable. Remembering it is important, because it is often used in project planning or when training for life-or-death situations.

The command-and-control element or C2 in a military organization or on an EP detail can be defined as *the exercise of authority and direction by a properly designated commanding officer over assigned and attached forces in the accomplishment of the mission.* As the Sentinel in your circle, you are your own C2 element. You are therefore in charge of planning.

As discussed elsewhere, we never plan to fail but we do fail to plan. The Sentinel must formulate a plan regardless of the *mission.* Whether picking the kiddies up from school or driving to the drugstore, we should follow simple planning procedures. The military uses Troop Leading Procedures as a format to follow when planning simple to complex missions.

In the military, troop leading is the procedure leaders use to prepare their units to accomplish a tactical mission. It begins when the leader is alerted for a mission. It starts over when the leader receives a change or a new mission.

In combat, rarely will leaders have enough time to go through each step in detail. Nor will you in your day-to-day routine. Leaders must use the procedure as outlined, if only in abbreviated form, to ensure that nothing is left out of planning and preparation and that their soldiers (your principal) understand the mission and prepare adequately. They continuously update their estimates throughout the preparation phase and adjust their plans as appropriate.

Please bear with the military format. I will conclude this chapter with a realistic practical application. Siphon through it and utilize what you need. Anytime you read the word *Leader*, you are reading your name.

Troop-Leading Procedures

Step 1. Receive the mission.
Step 2. Issue a warning order.
Step 3. Make a tentative plan.
Step 4. Start necessary movement.
Step 5. Reconnoiter.
Step 6. Complete the plan.
Step 7. Issue the complete order.
Step 8. Supervise.

1. Receive the Mission.

You might receive the mission as a weather warning, a local evacuation order, a news alert, or a bad feeling. You need to immediately begin to analyze it using the factors the military calls METT-T (mission, enemy, terrain and weather, troops and support available, time available):

- What is the *mission?* (Evacuate, batten down the hatches, etc.)
- What is known about the *enemy?* (Weather, traffic, intruders, obstructive policies, etc.)
- How will *terrain* and weather affect the operation?
- What *troops* are available? (Who can you call on for help?)
- How much *time* is available? (Is there a deadline, further danger approaching, etc.?)

You should use no more than one-third of the available time for your planning and issuing the "operation order." The remaining two-thirds is for *subordinates* to plan and prepare for the operation.

Leaders should also consider other factors such as available daylight and travel time to and from orders and rehearsals. In the offense, the leader has one-third of the time from his receipt of the mission to the unit's departure time. In the defense, the leader has one-third of the time from mission receipt to the time the squad or platoon must be prepared to defend.

In scheduling preparation activities, the leader should work backward from the LD or defend time. This is reverse planning. He or she must allow enough time for the completion of each task.

2. Issue a warning order.

The leader provides initial instructions in a warning order. The warning order contains enough information to begin preparation as soon as possible. Platoon SOPs should prescribe who will attend all warning orders and the actions they must take upon receipt. For example, drawing ammunition, rations, and water, and checking communications equipment.

The warning order has no specific format. One technique is to use the five-paragraph OPORD format. The leader issues the warning order with all the information he or she has available at the time. He or she provides updates as often as necessary. Never wait for more information before you start getting people moving.

If available, the following information may be included in a warning order:

- The mission or nature of the operation
- Who is participating in the operation
- Time of the operation
- Time and place for issuance of the operation order

3. Make a tentative plan.

The leader develops an estimate of the situation to use as the basis for his tentative plan. The estimate is the military decision-making process. It consists of five steps:

1. Detailed mission analysis
2. Situation analysis and course-of-action development
3. Analysis of each course of action

4.   Comparison of each course of action
5.   Decision

The decision represents the tentative plan. The leader updates the estimate continuously and refines his plan accordingly. He or she uses this plan as the starting point for coordination, reconnaissance, task organization (if required), and movement instructions. The leader works through this problem-solving sequence in as much detail as time allows. As the basis of his or her estimate, the leader considers the factors of METT-T (mission, enemy, terrain and weather, troops and support available, time available).

4. Start the necessary movement.
You family might have to start evacuating or making other changes while you are still organizing or making phone calls. Your spouse or partner or one of the older kids might have to direct everyone to task without your involvement. This should be understood.

This is where your subordinate leaders prepare men, weapons, and equipment for the coming mission. It is an excellent time for them to eat, conduct maintenance on weapons/equipment, and gather together anything they are going to need for the upcoming mission.

This step could occur at any time during the troop-leading procedure.

5. Reconnoiter.
If time allows, the leader makes a personal reconnaissance to verify his terrain analysis, adjust his plan, confirm the usability of routes, and time any critical movements. When time does not allow, the leader must make a map

reconnaissance. The leader must consider the risk inherent in conducting reconnaissance forward of friendly lines. Sometimes the leader must rely on others (for example, scouts) to conduct the reconnaissance if the risk of contact with the enemy is high.

6. Complete the plan.

The leader completes his plan based on the reconnaissance and any changes in the situation. The leader should review his or her mission, as received from his or her commander, to ensure that his or her plan meets the requirements of the mission and stays within the framework of the commander's intent.

7. Issue the complete order.

Platoon and squad leaders normally issue oral operations orders.

1. To aid subordinates in understanding the concept for the mission, leaders should issue the order within sight of the objective or on the defensive terrain. When this is not possible, they should use a terrain model or sketch.
2. Leaders must ensure that subordinates understand the mission, the commander's intent, the concept of the operation, and their assigned tasks. Leaders might require subordinates to repeat all or part of the order or demonstrate on the model or sketch, their understanding of the operation. They should also quiz their soldiers to ensure that all soldiers understand the mission.

8. Supervise.

The leader supervises the unit's preparation for combat by conducting rehearsals and inspections.

You will probably never have to lead a ranger patrol. The troop-leading procedures format, however, can assist you in your planning of day-to-day activities. Here is an example;

Step 1.   Receive the mission. *"Dad, will you take us to the state fair?"*

Step 2.   Issue a warning order. *"Yes, I will."*

Step 3.   Make a tentative plan. *"Let's go on Saturday."*

Step 4.   Start necessary movement. *"I will 'gas-up' the Suburban and have it ready to go."*

Step 5.   Reconnoiter. *Check the lay of the land on Google Earth. Look for parking and a hotel nearby.*

Step 6.   Complete the plan. *Make a hotel reservation. Buy tickets in advance. Stop at an ATM*

Step 7.   Issue the complete order. *"Kids, we will leave on Friday after school. We will stay the night at a hotel nearby. We will get to the fair as soon as the gates open on Saturday. Pack a day bag."*

Step 8.   Supervise. *"Behave yourselves, pay attention and have fun!"*

Use the World Wide Web

Where would we be without the Internet? Some might say, "Better off without it." For others, it has become an absolute necessity. Regardless, it is the here and now.

Check and update your computer software, including Windows operating systems (and others like Mac OS) and Web browsers. Threats from viruses and attackers often take advantage of vulnerabilities in these software packages. Most vendors offer ways for customers to keep their software up-to-date. Contact the software vendor directly to access any available updates.

Install antivirus/antispyware software to protect your computer and detect and remove viruses. Make sure your software is up-to-date, because new viruses appear daily. Your antivirus/antispyware software is only as good as its last update. Contact the software vendor directly to access available updates.

Install software for spam-filtering and spam-blocking. Some antivirus/antispyware software packages include these features. Check with your software vendor for the features available with your software.

Be wary of e-mail offers that come from a source you don't recognize. If you believe an e-mail is fraudulent, don't reply to the e-mail, click any links within the e-mail, or open any attachments.

Be wary of any e-mail or popup messages declaring your accounts in jeopardy or asking for personal information.

Scammers typically use scare tactics to get people to react immediately.

Do not respond to *spammed* e-mails, those sent to a multitude of random addresses. If an e-mail seems suspicious, don't even click the link asking to be taken off the sender's list. A response only confirms the accuracy of your e-mail address and may result in even more messages filling up your inbox. (One way to avoid getting spam is to not post your e-mail address to chat rooms, instant-message services, Internet bulletin boards, and newsgroups.)

Never submit your credit card details or other personal information on non-secure websites. Before submitting your user name and password to log on, make sure your browser window displays the closed padlock symbol and the URL (the online address) begins with "https://" only. Secure web pages show a locked padlock icon that appears in yellow or in a yellow box at the bottom of the Web browser screen.

Never share your user names and passwords or store them on your computer.

Be cautious when using shared or public computers (including those used by roommates or others at your home, as well as those at libraries, Internet cafés, hotels, and schools). You don't know what may be installed on these computers. Public computers are traditionally on open networks and can be susceptible to monitoring without your knowledge.

Whenever you have accessed sensitive account information online, log off the website and close your Web browser before going to other online sites.

Be smart about your password. The best passwords are ones that are difficult to guess. Try using a password that consists of a combination of numbers, letters, upper and lower case, punctuation, and special characters. You should change your password regularly and use a different password for each of your accounts. Don't share your password with others and never reply to *phishing* emails—those looking to get information from you—with your password or other sensitive information.

It bears repeating: don't store your passwords on your computer. If you need to write down your passwords, store them in a secure, private place.

Use extra caution with wireless connections. Wireless networks might not provide as much security as wired Internet connections. In fact, many *hotspots*—wireless networks in public areas like airports, hotels and restaurants—reduce their security so that it's easier for individuals to access and use these wireless networks. Unless you use a security *token*, you might decide that accessing your online brokerage account through a wireless connection isn't worth the security risk.

The Web is not only a place where your security can be breached, it can also be used to increase your security level. There are several credible sites that search crime and credit records, offer background checks and reverse phone number look-ups. For a minimum fee, you can get near-instant feedback, which can offer great peace of mind when checking on a new nanny.

Security Is in Numbers

When it comes to your protection detail, there are assets and there are liabilities. Your kids do not have to be liabilities.

Kids are pretty perceptive and possess keen intellect beyond their experience. You can increase your kids' skills of perception and observation by playing certain "Look and Report" games. These games will have a direct impact on their own security but will remain in their minds merely a game.

My disaster planning starts in the WalMart parking lot. I say this in jest, but huge parking lots can be precarious.

"Heads on a swivel!" I will call out to my kids as we pull into a parking lot. "Parking lots are dangerous," I will continue, "so keep a lookout!" Then I might add as we approach a department store, "You lead the way."

Once we exit, we will take turns asking questions:

"What color was the car that stopped and let us pass?"

"What was the cashier's name?"

"How many people were in line in front of us?"

"What was the boy's name who was being scolded by his mom?"

"What dropped and made the loud noise near the electronics department?"

These are just some examples of questions we might ask. They are neither subjective nor too ambiguous.

Another thing kids are switched on to, because it's fun, is military jargon. This jargon works well for the military as it reduces chaos and encourages order. This is the same behavior you would want to instill in your family in a busy place like, say . . . an amusement park. Big place with lots of hustle and bustle.

Straight out of the US Army Ranger Handbook, we can pull phrases that directly relate to the mission at hand. In this particular case, the mission is to stay safe and have fun.

The phraseology starts in the parking lot by introducing the Rally Point (RP). A rally point is a place designated by the military leader where the platoon moves to reassemble and reorganize if it becomes dispersed.

The most common types of rally points are objective, initial, en route, reentry, and near and far side. Soldiers must know which rally point to move to at each phase of the patrol mission. They should know what actions are required there and how long they are to wait at each rally point before moving to another.

The **objective rally point** (ORP) is a point out of sight, sound, and small-arms range of the objective area. It is normally located in the direction that the platoon plans to move after completing its actions on the objective. The ORP is tentative until the objective is pinpointed. In this particular case, the car in the parking lot is the ORP.

An **initial rally point** is a place inside of friendly lines where a unit may assemble and reorganize if it makes enemy contact during the departure of friendly lines or before reaching the first en-route rally point. It is normally selected by the commander of the friendly unit. In our case of the amusement park, this might be the ticket booth at the park's entrance.

The leader designates **en-route rally points** based on the terrain, vegetation, and visibility. Any feature that stands out and can be seen from a distance will work, such as the Ferris wheel ticket booth.

The **reentry rally point** is located out of sight, sound, and small-arms weapons range of the friendly unit through which the platoon will return. This also means that the RRP should be outside the final protective fires of the friendly unit. The platoon occupies the RRP as a security perimeter. Any prominent terrain feature can be used here—a snack bar, say.

Near and far rally points are on the near and far side of danger areas. If the platoon makes contact while crossing the danger area and control is lost, soldiers on either side move to the rally point nearest them. They establish security, reestablish the chain of command, determine their personnel and equipment status, continue the patrol mission, and link up at the ORP.

Before departing the ORP, the kids will be assigned a *Safe Pocket* in which is kept a business card of the parent in charge and any other information needed to assist friendly forces with reestablishing linkup in the event of a break in contact.

The kids will know cardinal directions (i.e., north, south, east, and west) to make it easier to orient themselves. They will also know *clock direction*—"restroom at three o'clock"—so that we can communicate as to who has who's *six* or rear security.

If we really want to get gung-ho, we might issue a five-paragraph operations' order:

- Situation.
- Mission.
- Execution.
- Command and signal.
- Service and support.

Or a five-point contingency plan: who, what, where, when, and why.

Before departing the ORP, the kids will be reminded to keep their heads on a swivel.

You now have a force to be reckoned with. You are on your way to creating a cohesive team of assets instead of liabilities.

Better to Have . . .

Yes, *it's better to have and not need than to need
and not have.*

In Carthage, North Carolina, a town that neighbors my
town, March 29, 2009, is a date to remember. It was a warm
sunny Sunday. The sky was clear in this southern town of
two thousand people, and the lone on-duty police officer,
twenty-five-year-old Justin Garner, was observing traffic
trickle toward church.

At about ten a.m., the Moore County 911 dispatcher
disturbed the Norman Rockwell–like setting with a report,
"Shot's fired at 801 Pinehurst Avenue."

Justin, a four-and-a-half-year veteran of the Carthage
Police Department steered his Dodge Charger patrol car
toward the Pine Lake Health and Rehab Center for the elderly.
His mind had not yet wrapped itself around the possibility
that someone might be shooting inside the facility. Calls of
this type were usually hunters mistakenly getting too close
to town. When he rolled into the lot at the facility, a red Ford
Ranger caught his attention. It had the driver's side window
shot out, and he knew something more serious was in store
for him on this call than disoriented hunters.

Suddenly a woman came running to the door and
exclaimed that there was a man inside and "He is shooting

123

people!" By the frantic look on her face, she did not have to add, "This is not a drill."

Justin Garner, who was the only officer on duty in Carthage, entered the rehab center. He was met with dead silence. He later said, "You could have heard a pin drop." As he moved further into the facility, he could see no one near the front door other than an elderly woman in a wheel chair. When he checked on her, he could see she had been shot in the chest. "She was gone," Justin recalled quietly, moved by the haunting image, "I saw there were elderly residents wandering about the facility, who did not have a clue what was happening. I knew that someone was shooting them and could not figure out why anyone would shoot them. They were like children . . . defenseless. I thought, *I had to find this guy*," said Justin.

He reached the nurse's station, and other than disoriented elderly patients, he saw nothing and heard nothing to indicate where the gunman was. He instinctively stepped into one hallway and paused. Then he heard shots, and the gunman appeared straight down the hallway he was in.

The suspect, Robert Stewart, was carrying a 12-gauge shotgun and had a bag filled with ammunition strapped over his shoulder. He possessed a revolver in a holster slipped in the middle of his back, and he was hunting for his ex-wife, who was working in a locked-down facility at the rehab center.

He had not found her, and for some reason had chosen to shoot anyone he met. At the moment he turned to face Officer Garner, eight innocents lay dead and there were two more wounded. Stewart was determined there would be more killings, and Justin was determined to end the violence in this, the most desperate moment of his life.

Justin raised and aimed his .40 caliber Glock 22. Stewart was loading shells into his shotgun, and Justin shouted for him to "drop the weapon!" three times. Stewart turned, shouldered his weapon and brought it down to bear on Justin. At the same moment, Justin fired once. Officer Garner did not hear his weapon fire and did not hear Stewart's weapon fire, but he knew Stewart had.

Justin felt a sharp sudden burning in his leg and foot, but instinctively moved into a doorway for cover. He was concerned Stewart might be advancing on him, so he leaned out and saw Stewart was down and not moving. Justin had fired once and hit Stewart in the chest, incapacitating him.

He recalled, "I felt the burning in my leg, but it did not really, really hurt. I was still able to walk up and cuff the man."

In the initial scan of the area, it appeared the suspect was alone and conscious, but not moving. He had dropped the shotgun, but Justin found the revolver and removed it from Stewart's holster, unloaded it, and slid it out of reach.

From the time of the call to the time Justin calmly reported that shots had been fired and the suspect was down, four minutes had elapsed. He told dispatch that he was also wounded.

I decided to add this news piece as a finisher because Officer Garner had at that time the qualities needed to be the Sentinel: *Attitude, aptitude, and desire.*

You too possess the ability to be the lord of your own domain. You can count on yourself to protect your own life and the lives of those close to you. Become your family's agent of correction. Become the Sentinel.

About the Author

Pat McNamara (Mac) has twenty-two years of special-operations experience. He was a member of a special-missions unit for thirteen years. He has extensive experience in hostile fire/combat zones in the Middle East and Eastern Europe. He was depended on to train individuals at basic and advanced levels of marksmanship and combat tactics with emphasis on IED IADs in support of the GWOT (global war on terror).

As his unit's marksmanship NCO, Mac developed his own marksmanship club with the National Rifle Association's civilian marksmanship program and affiliations of the United States Practical Shooting Association. He ran monthly IPSC matches and ran semiannual military marksmanship championships to encourage marksmanship fundamentals and competitiveness throughout the army.

Mac has been a competitive shooter for over twenty years and has competed at the top levels in both military and civilian competitions and was a member of his unit's first-place team in the International Counter-Terrorism Olympics. His other marksmanship achievements include overall winner of the 2004 All-Army Small Arms Championships, and he is a U.S. Army Distinguished Pistol Shot.

SGM McNamara was his unit's primary advanced pistol and rifle marksmanship instructor for two years. In addition, he instructed advanced close-quarter battle techniques, concealed weapons employment, high-speed motorcade and non-motorcade driving techniques, mountain and urban climbing, basic and advanced demolitions, advanced explosive entry techniques, and was its primary hand-combat instructor, rewriting the preexisting POI.

Mac owns and runs his own performance-based training business, TMACS INC.